Did You Boscov Today?

A tribute to our grandfather,
as told by those who knew and loved him.

Albert Boscov
1929-2017

Compiled and edited by
Amelia Xanthe Boscov, Jonah Boscov-Brown, and Josh Aichenbaum

Illustrated by Abby Ryder and Jessica Santucci

Printed in Reading, PA
by R•E•P Commercial Printing

ISBN: 978-0-9961558-1-6

Artwork by Abby Ryder and Jess Santucci,
artists at the GoggleWorks Center for the Arts

Layout by Randall Brown

This book is a work of nonfiction. All stories within represent the
storytellers' memories of Albert Boscov.

To our grandmother

For every story where you're off screen,
behind the scenes,
We know you held his hand.
For every family photo where you're unseen,
You held the camera.
You raised three girls,
who raised us.
You are his
forever darling sweetheart,
his honey bunny...
our Eunie.

MEMO from *Albert R. Boscov*, from 1976

Who says there's no customer loyalty.

Will you be my friend? I know it's presumptuous. We don't know each other. Even though we've just met I sense I like you, and I'm going to try to make you like me! Call it Sales Promotion. Call it Public Relations. Call it Image. I prefer to call it by its real name... SUCCESS.

Retailers often tell me that there's no customer loyalty anymore. In the words of the immortal Samuel Johnson...THAT'S BS... (Bad Sales)!

It's difficult to be loyal to nothing...or to price alone, for if your loyalty is to price alone, then your loyalty can be sought for a dime. In my stores, I believe achieving customer loyalty is as important as good merchandising.

I'd like to tell you how we achieve it at Boscov's. In April, we ran a promotion called Did You Boscov Today. It started as a joke about seven years ago. Easter fell in March, and we wondered how to make those huge April figures. We decided we would offer any customer a set of Revere or Corning Ware absolutely FREE if she visited Boscov's 26 times in April. (That's every single shopping day). We expected a few hundred...we got 17,000. There was no purchase required, but if one shopped at Boscov's 26 times a month, there wasn't much time to shop anywhere else, and April became our second-largest month of the year.

It was important to make Boscoving fun, not a chore. To achieve this, we mixed contests, special events, and lots of surprises with the daily visits.

Writing Boscov graffiti plays a big part. Our customers are invited to write silly slogans, using Boscov as a verb. For instance, "I could have Boscoved all night," or "Boscov with a Friend" and "Wine, Women, and Boscov's."

Many of these slogans are printed in our newspaper ads.

The authors win cash prizes, and our ads become popular reading, and everyone chuckles. We also print the best slogans on pressure sensitive stickers, and our customers plaster the city. At the validation booth, customers help themselves to buttons with the crazy slogans printed on them.

Of course, our bags ask, "Did You Boscov Today," as do our stationary and the placemats in our Country Kitchens, and those

same four words, "Did You Boscov Today," pop up on coasters in neighborhood bars and popular night spots. And those aren't the only places the slogan appears.

Would you believe the slogan appears on T-Shirts, baby diapers, flags, neckties, trousers, cakes, toilet paper, and on the rear of our elegant fashion models? The whole town talks Boscoving in April, and we have an opportunity to make friends. The customers get to know our store, our co-workers, and our merchandise...and we make sure we're at our best.

Let's take a look at some other friend-makers....

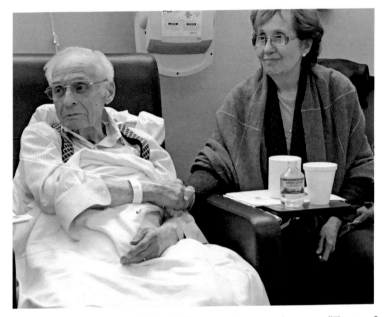

On February 10th, 2017, Al Boscov's last words were, "Eunie, I love you."

He passed away from pancreatic cancer at the age of 87, held by his wife, Eunice, and by his three girls, Ruth, Ellen, and Meg, who curled up in the bed next to him and held him in their arms. Ruth is my mother and the oldest of the three sisters.

To borrow a turn of phrase from my grandfather, "Will you be my friend?"

I know we hardly know each other, but I'd like to share an

uplifting story with you.

As with most uplifting stories, it doesn't begin with bluebirds singing, "What a wonderful day..." In early January, 2017, my mom called me and told me of my grandfather's diagnosis. I don't think we or he ever thought he would die.

If you don't know anything about him, Al Boscov was the Energizer bunny of retail. He was a gentle giant at five feet five inches tall, the last real merchant, a mensch, and so much more, but to me and my cousins, he was and always has been our "Granddaddy Al" (or "Daddy Al" for short).

My mom's instructions had been simple: "Come home when you can. Granddaddy needs somebody to drive him to work."

My grandfather spent his life giving workaholics a good name, and he wasn't going to stop now.

Before she hung up, my mom added, as if it were a special surprise, "Aunt Meggie is buying you a chauffeur's hat."

The Boscovs' unofficial family motto is "Life is short and silly!" Half of that motto we have no choice but to live by. The tallest Boscov grandchild is a giant at five feet eight inches small. The other half of that motto we embrace fully. Family dinners are accompanied by impromptu dances, songs, and the best cringe-worthy puns. Only a Boscov would learn of a cancer diagnosis and go shopping, and only a Boscov would shop for a costume (a chauffeur's hat, no less) for their nephew in an effort to take life's unpredictability, its hardships, and its cruel twists of fate and turn them into positives.

Proudly wearing the chauffeur's hat, I arrived in Reading,

Pennsylvania a week later. Our first stop was the Reading Hospital. I proudly ran around my grandfather's car to open the passenger door for him.

It wasn't until we entered the hospital, and I saw my brother waiting, and the hospital's routine took us from one room to the next, that the gravity of the situation hit me. My mom and granddaddy proudly call themselves "Crybabies." I wish I were. More often, I'm bottled up until I'm suddenly not. I took off the hat because I felt silly, crying in a chauffeur's hat. For a few days, I carried it around with me. I thought if I could live by the family motto and be silly and wear the hat, then I would have done my job. But I lost it. Or misplaced it. I'm not sure where the chauffeur hat is today.

What has lasted with me from that week is the memory of my grandfather's heroism. He was 87; he had cancer, type two diabetes, and the normal mix of maladies that go along with being older. And yet, every day he requested a seven o' clock wake-up call—if not earlier—so he could work. Every day, he sang or whistled while he showered. I—or more often my brother—sat on the edge of the bathtub and waited to hand him a towel. His feet were encased in the type of plastic bags you wear with a broken leg. We removed them and dried his feet, which were bandaged and swollen, caused by his non-functioning liver and its build-up of bilirubin.

We helped him put on his socks. He would say, 'Thank you, Joshie," and "Thank you, David" to my brother. I've never heard someone say thank you so many times in one week.

Whenever someone helped him, it was always, "Thank you,

Ruthie," "Thank you, Meggie," "Thank you, Ellen...."

In that one week, I learned how he dressed every day of his life. I learned how to use a shoehorn and how suspenders work. He taught me "nothing is impossible" and no problem impossible to solve.

When the bilirubin in his skin caused him to itch and robbed him of sleep, he put rubber bands on each long-sleeved pajama wrist so he wouldn't subconsciously lift and scratch. Sounds far-fetched but somehow, the rubber bands worked.

He did all of this behind closed doors, in the company of his family, who over-eagerly waited on him.

Every day, he walked into the Boscov's East store in a suit, tie, and suspenders, and he conducted business. Everyone saw him and his yellowing skin, and they were concerned for his health. He was more concerned with the well-being of everyone else around him.

In a meeting with a vendor, his eyes welled. The vendor had too recently lost his wife. The meeting involved some hardline goods that the vendor needed to sell.

I remember my grandfather saying, "There's no need to kill yourself over this, we're friends. If we're hurting you..." and the vendor insisted, "No, no, no," and gave the merchandise away at a more than reasonable price.

Their business was built on a long-lasting friendship.

The days passed. Yes, his health deteriorated. But his optimism was undying. When he could no longer travel to work, he brought work to him.

He worked even at the hospital, a Boscov basket of ads next to his bedside. After a long day, I remember him singing for the nurse's amusement (what follows is the censored version):

Bilirubin, you sonnuva *%@#
We're gonna get rid of this dang itch!

His humor helped his and our pain subside, if only momentarily. After a week, my brother David took over my chauffeur and assistant duties. He did the bulk of the heavy lifting, helping Granddaddy in and out of bed when Granddaddy could no longer lift himself.

At this point, I could see why you might be discouraged if not downright downtrodden. Maybe you're sensing the inevitability of how this story must end, knowing that he passed away on February,

10th, 2017, a month after learning of his diagnosis.

But never forget these words...

nothing is impossible

...and that his optimism truly is undying.

Amelia Xanthe Boscov

One day, while Granddaddy was in the hospital, my cousin Jonah and I drove to visit him. As we started the hour-long drive from Philly, I tried to remember the last time I had been to Reading.

Surely for a happier occasion: a holiday, a family dinner, maybe a birthday? Was it four years ago? Maybe longer?

I couldn't remember.

"I haven't been to Reading in forever."

Jonah said, "Me neither."

I thought about all the times Jonah, his sister Chloe, and I sat in the backseat, going to Reading as children. I had no idea in a few months, Jonah and I would be making the drive several times a week to put a book of memories together.

When we arrived to the Reading Hospital, my mom, aunts,

and grandma were already there. Despite the unfamiliar setting, our family was the same as always: laughing, occasionally singing, snacks strewn everywhere.

When everyone else went to get dinner, Jonah and I stayed in the room with Granddaddy. Soon the corners of Granddaddy's mouth turned down. "Three daughters," he said as his eyes filled with tears, "And five grandchildren." He patted our hands, "Not bad, not bad at all."

I stayed at home as long as I could, but soon, I had to go back to college. My mom would not only text me and call me with updates; she would also send pictures—pictures that I would later learn she also posted on Facebook. (At the time, I was ignoring social media).

After the memorial service, my cousin Josh asked if I'd like to help put together a book of memories about Granddaddy Al. I said I would love to help. Since I was ignoring social media, I had no idea what we were working with until Josh sent me a document of all the collected emails and condolence letters that had come in over the past few weeks. The love I felt through my computer screen was unbelievable. That is when I went back, and I looked at Facebook. There were thousands of comments on my mom's posts. As I read them, they made me feel not only love, but also community.

I quickly realized we would have no shortage of stories and memories for the book. Once Jonah and I got home from college and Josh returned from LA, we began to sort through all of the stories, and we collected more. We went to Boscov's East, Boscov's North, the Berkshire Mall, Wilkes Barre, Neshaminy, Coventry, Egg

Harbor Township, DirectLink, and to Our City Reading to hear from Granddaddy's friends and coworkers. We got to cry, laugh, and hug so many people, all while learning about our grandfather. Each day we drove to Reading, more memories came flooding back to me.

I remembered that the bumpy and twisty road to our grandparents' house, which now seemed like an unnecessarily hilly nuisance, was what Chloe, Jonah, and I used to call "roller-coaster road." It was always our favorite part of the long journey to our grandparents'— I couldn't believe I had forgotten the adventures of "roller-coaster road." Objects we'd find in Granddaddy's office or bedroom would spark a memory—the Father's Day when we gave him a teddy bear in a raincoat that sang "Singing in the Rain." Granddaddy danced and sang along with the music and put an arm around us, so we'd join him. As I picked up a toy horse I found in a closet, I could hear Granddaddy neighing and playing along with me.

When he died, I didn't think we'd get to experience any new stories with him. I felt like his cancer robbed us of stories we deserved. With every new memory people shared, we got to see, hear, and feel Granddaddy's spirit come alive again, and we were able to form an entire book from the experience.

Over the years, my cousins and I have learned so much from our grandfather. As we curated this book, we noticed the lessons he taught us when we were children recurred in the stories and, as we heard more and more stories, we learned new lessons that would have been lost on us otherwise. We knew what Granddaddy was like outside of work, but through everyone's memories, we began to see how he lived every day, every moment.

Our family (and I) have learned Boscov coworkers often wonder "What would Albert do?" The stories in this book will show you not only why we ask that question, but also how he lived.

The simple answer is he Boscov-ed, in the truest sense of the word.

Creating this book has given me so much. It has helped me come closer to "Boscov"-ing every day, and I hope that after you finish reading this book, you, too, will look back and ask yourself, "Did I Boscov today?"

Cindy Arbogast

Since 1988, I've worked in Travel in the Selinsgrove store. I met Albert in 1993 at Dorney Park. Our store was putting on a skit called "Chairman of the Board." We were promoting Boscov charges. I was on stage setting up, when a man in casual clothes and sneakers jumped up on stage and offered to help. He asked me where everything went, and I proceeded to tell him where the speakers went and then the microphones and signage. I thanked him for his help, and he jumped back down into the audience.

We performed our skit and afterward enjoyed the park and the food until it was time to go. The next day, a coworker said to me something like, "I saw you telling Al Boscov what to do yesterday."

I said, "You did?"

"Yeah, that was Al Boscov who set up your skit."

He was such a nice down-to-earth guy.

Cass Cutrufelli

In early 2000 I was a secretary for Dr. Lloyd Norman (Vice Principal at Reading High School). One day Mr. Boscov came in to see Dr. Norman regarding his speaking engagement at Reading High School.

At that time, Dr. Norman introduced me to Mr. Boscov and told him how much I loved shopping at Boscov's East. Mr. Boscov was so happy that he kneeled down on one knee and kissed my hand. I will never forget his kindness and humility.

Shannon Miller

My fondest memory took place in Boscov's East, 2015. I was walking the hallway downstairs. A stock boy was pushing a cart. Mr. Boscov was also walking the hall and asked the stock boy to stop. He hopped on top of the cart and said, "Push me!" It took some convincing to get the stock boy to actually push Mr. Boscov. But down the hall they went, with Mr. Boscov surfing on the cart. Everyone within eyesight was laughing and cheering them on. I am happy to say I was in that hallway and saw such a joyous and happy Mr. Boscov.

Kim Gormley

During the pre-opening days of the Salisbury store, Mr. Boscov decided that he was so impressed with the work that the visual department had done that he wanted to treat us to lunch. Mr. B suggested we take his car, so we all walked outside and there it was...

his old, wood-paneled station wagon. We piled in, one on top of the other, laying down in the back, sitting on top of each other's laps, looking like a clown car, and perhaps breaking some laws.

But we were off and running.

Lunch was wonderful, and we ate more than our fill, but then it was time to pile back in...oops! We shoved back in the station wagon. After a bit of groaning, we were on our way.

Waiting in front of the store was Mr. B.

When he saw the mess of us in the car, he couldn't stop laughing. He helped us unpile ourselves, and we all thanked him.

Every time I see a wood-paneled station wagon, I laugh, remembering our adventure and my wonderful boss.

Joe Ricards

About ten years ago, we had an advertising meeting in the conference room. This was my first meeting with the team. Mr. B came in and started speaking while walking around the table.

He stopped behind my chair. I then felt his hands on my shoulders. He started massaging me.

I know my face turned a bit red. It felt great! He then leaned in and kissed my bald head. The man is a legend—such great wit and charm.

Doug Messinger

My favorite story about Albie was told to me by Don Helms. Don Helms was the head of visual merchandise for Boscov's in the 1970s. Albie was downstairs in the East auditorium during a Christmastime toy extravaganza. There were a hundred kids and their parents playing with the toys. Albie was sitting on a high stool, talking to Don while wearing Mickey Mouse ears, when the VP of Marketing from Bigelow carpets came over to talk business. After five minutes, Albie realized that he was still wearing the ears, looked at the man as if to say "so sorry," and touching the ears, called out to his assistant, "Can you bring another pair of these?"

I love that story because it illustrates his unique humor, humble confidence, and charismatic inclusiveness.

Michael Freiman

About ten years ago, I was eating lunch at a merchandising event with Albert. We spoke about brands, business, and families. I mentioned how a few of my brands are family-owned and made in America. He immediately looked up and said, "So am I!"

When I was a kid, my sisters and I would beg our dad to tell us stories from when he was growing up. I remember our family taking long drives to Atlantic City where we vacationed. On the ride, either Ruth, Meg, or I would say, "Tell us a story."

Once one of us did, we all chimed in, "Tell us a story, Dad, a story!"

He loved telling stories, so we got to hear his stories again and again. Maybe you've heard stories about how my father liked to get on the floor and play with kids. In his storytelling, he was the same way. He always found a way to get on our level and relate to us.

He told us about his father Solomon Boscov, who we knew as Poppy. Poppy was a short man—only four foot eleven. Poppy thought he was so small because he didn't get enough nutrition growing up in Russia, so he insisted that all four of his children eat properly.

Every day, all four Boscov children lined up from oldest to youngest with spoons. First came the eldest Boscov, which was Joe, with his spoon held dutifully forward, followed by his sisters, Shirley and Reba, and lastly, followed by Dad, who back then was little Albert.

Poppy served them spoonfuls of cod liver oil because, back then, they thought cod liver oil was healthy. One day, little Albert decided he was sick of Poppy's healthy diet. When it was his turn, he held up a fork instead, and Poppy accidentally poured the oil all over the floor. The way my father told it, Poppy practically turned into a cartoon character. Poppy exclaimed, "Why, you!" and he chased

him all around the store.

Another story Dad liked to tell was about the flies. One of his first jobs at the store was catching flies. Poppy gave him a dime for every fifty flies he caught. That dime was enough for Dad to buy ice cream or to go to the movies. It was a really good job if he could

only catch the flies. But flies are difficult to catch!

After a while, Dad realized that a week-old dead fly looked exactly like a newly caught dead fly, so he started recycling them. The story goes that he got caught with the counterfeit flies, and Poppy taught him a lesson about integrity. But that's not how I remember it!

When I was a kid, I think Dad left out the moral. What I remember is little Albert getting away with sneaking dead flies and getting away with all of his fun. Maybe I'm misremembering it.

But in his stories, Dad was always a lovable trickster, and I think that's why we loved hearing his stories so much. Because they were fun.

as remembered by Albert's sister, Shirley Holzman in 1993

When my little brother was five, he had a friend named Curtis Wright, and Curtis had a lot of wonderful toys. One day, Albert convinced Curtis of a great idea. They set up shop on Curtis' front porch, where they proceeded to sell all of Curtis' wonderful toys at a fifty-fifty split.

That was Albert's first real attempt at being an entrepreneur.

At age twelve, my brother decided he wanted a paper route. Our parents agreed he could have a morning route, but that didn't satisfy him; before we knew it, Albert also had the evening route, and this was all while he was also helping at the store. All four of us started working at the store at a young age. But Albert did even more. By the time he was in his early teens, he was our father's partner. Sometimes he played tricks on our father and the coworkers. He would take a pen and mark down the merchandise—very often below cost.

Bob Brok

Albert's father Solomon Boscov came to America from Russia in 1911. He was a peddler, traveling by foot and then by horse-and-buggy. His first store was called Economy Shoe and Dry Goods, which Albert would later rename Boscov's. Little by little, the store grew. Every few years, Solomon knocked down the wall into the adjacent rowhouse, expanding until the store took up a total of four rowhouses.

In the mid-1920s, Solomon was doing well at the store and decided to invest in real estate. My father bought one of Solomon's houses. When the Depression hit, some people could no longer afford their mortgage, so a few of the houses returned to Solomon. The Boscov family moved from house to house until they could sell them, and that's how Albert and I ended up as neighbors. The house next to ours opened up. The Boscov family moved in.

As with most stories with Albert, the story of how Albert and I became lifelong friends involves food. Albert's mother always cooked chicken, all types of chicken, but always chicken, and my mother made pot roast and mashed potatoes, with gravy and meringue pie. Albert started hanging out at our place. He was the kind of kid everyone liked. If he didn't show up at dinnertime, my mother

would wonder, "Where could Albert be?"

Albert's older brother was my age, but somehow I ended up spending more time with Al. Al was born September 22, 1929. I was born in September 1921. Even though he was half our age, my friends didn't mind if he tagged along because he was such a nice kid.

We developed a routine.

A gang of us would hang out, and Albert was one of us. We would steal apples and grapes from a neighbor's tree and then hitchhike with 22 rifles to Leesport, where we would shoot rats at the dump. Then we would gather bottles and throw them into the creek where we would watch them float down the stream and shoot them. I'm amazed nobody ever complained.

Another game we played took place on the rooftop of our houses. We would go on the roof with a paper bag and a water bottle. When someone walked by, we poured water into the bag, folded the top, and threw it so it would land right behind the pedestrian. We would lie flat on the roof and hear a lot of new words.

One day Albie misjudged and hit his target in the head. Well, that was the end of that game!

When I was in high school, I had a party at my house for a few friends my age.

Eight-year-old Albert was there to help my mom serve the food. When the party ended, a girl from Mt. Penn needed a ride home, so I got permission to use the family car. As I was getting our coats, Albie suggested he could ride along. I helped the girl into the front seat. As we started out on Hampden Blvd, I noticed that the girl was sliding closer and closer to me. I thought that was great. By the time we reached City Park, she was almost touching me. I stopped for a red light, glanced over, and noticed a little arm around her shoulder. Both my hands were still on the steering wheel! She never realized little Albie was in the car with us.

I often think of the many things I taught him as a kid, all certainly of questionable worth. Yet he went on to do more good deeds in Reading than anyone since William Penn.

Albie and I shared eighty years of friendship. For those of us who were fortunate enough to know him and for those of us fortunate enough to have been impacted by his generosity and caring nature, we probably can all agree that we were given a wondrous gift just in knowing him.

Shirley Boscov

When I was engaged to Albert's older brother Joe, Albert was only fourteen. My parents made a little engagement party for us. I didn't know Albert well at the time. We were all sitting in my mother's apartment on the couch, and Albert sat next to me and kept giving me butterfly kisses, when you flutter your eyelashes against another person's cheek. It was so funny, all night long, I

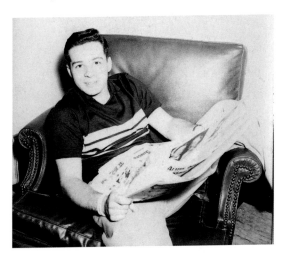

was sitting next to Albie, the butterfly. He wouldn't leave my side.

Albert grew up, but he never lost that sweetness.

When Albert started running the business, I remember Joe telling Albert, "Don't be afraid to hire someone smarter than you."

Later on, Joe was instrumental in getting Albert to form a board. Albert didn't think he needed one, but Joe encouraged him. He told him that you can learn from other people.

success is never one person

Steve Bonner

Back when there were only a few stores, every store came up with a skit at the employee picnic. One of the most memorable skits was a two man show, where someone dressed up as Albert, and another co-worker dressed up Al's business partner, Ed Lakin. The coworker playing Albert entered with a basket of money and skipped while throwing dollar bills into the air. The coworker playing Ed trailed behind him and picked up all of the cash, one dollar at a time. That was a good skit! It really captured their relationship.

Peter Lakin

Before he joined the company, my father Ed Lakin worked for an accounting firm in New York. He also happened to be married to a Boscov. Reba Boscov was the second youngest of Solomon and Ethel Boscov's four children, (Albert being the youngest). Ethel insisted that my dad join the family business because she didn't like her daughter living so far away from home. Back then, the family business really was just a corner store on 9th and Pike Street. But Ethel got her way. Her daughter returned to Reading, and my father became business partners with Albert, a relationship that lasted them over a half century. I think my dad and Albert complemented each other very well.

Every day, my dad ate five M&Ms from a jar in his office—no more. Albert, on the other hand, would eat a handful at a time. I

guess my dad was a moderating influence on Albert, or at least he tried to be. He oversaw the store's finances and operations, whereas Albert was the marketing wiz. I can imagine Albert telling a buyer to "buy more" and my dad telling the same buyer "less" while working with the buyer to evaluate how much merchandise to purchase.

Their relationship and dynamic were slightly more complicated than my dad being the numbers guy and Albert doing promotions. Each one of them knew every aspect of the company inside and out. They built the store together from the very beginning and had so much respect for each other. They spent so many years in business, and even more as family. So many years together, but I never saw them not get along. I think that says a lot about their partnership and friendship.

When we were children, my dad would take my sisters and me to the neighborhood in Reading where he grew up. As we walked, he told us stories about his father, who we called Poppy.

He would tell us, "Your Poppy used to take me for walks on the same road where we're walking now. He would point at the rowhouses and tell us that the man who lived in the first rowhouse lost it and his wife because he drank, and the man in the neighboring house coughed himself to death because he smoked. That's how Poppy taught me 'don't drink, don't smoke,' or it will ruin your life."

It was a very creative way for our dad to teach us a lesson that his father taught him. Poppy was a big influence on our father.

The most important lesson Poppy taught him was to, "Give back to this country. Because it has given us everything."

My sisters and I didn't really understand what that meant, so Dad explained, "Your Nanny and your Poppy met right here in Reading, PA, but they were both originally from Russia. In Russia, back then, things were bad for Jewish people. They didn't have the same rights as non-Jews.

"They had to live in Jewish ghettos, and there was violence against them. Like in *Fiddler on the Roof*. Nanny and Poppy, when

they were very young adults, had to leave Russia for their own safety. Unfortunately, most of our family didn't get out."

Dad got teary-eyed. He then smiled at us and said, "Poppy was very grateful to this country and the opportunities it gave him. He liked to tell us about his adventures as a new immigrant."

My sisters and I liked hearing those stories, too. As we walked together through Dad's old neighborhood, Dad would tell us stories about Poppy.

Dad told us how Poppy came to the US with only twenty dollars in his pocket. Folks told Poppy, "Go to Washington DC because everyone drinks lemonade in Washington."

So Poppy went to Washington, and he invested his twenty dollars on lemons. Soon he discovered people in Washington D.C. weren't so thirsty for lemonade.

Then Poppy was told, "Go to Reading PA because everyone there speaks Yiddish."

After arriving in Reading, Poppy soon discovered people spoke Pennsylvania Dutch and English—not Yiddish. Poppy could understand just enough Pennsylvania Dutch to ask for some English lessons.

One time, Dad stopped walking and said, "After many more adventures, Poppy saved up enough money to start a little Boscov's." And Dad showed us, "It was right here." He said, "This is where the first Boscov's used to be—right here on 9th and Pike."

Dad used to say that what he wanted most in life was to make his father proud.

Patt Pizzi

My mother worked for Solomon Boscov at the 9th and Pike street store when Albert and his siblings were little kids. When I came to work for Boscov's twenty-some years later, Solomon was a sweet old man. One day, I cleared out the upstairs warehouse. I couldn't get to the dump in time, so the truck was parked out front. When I came back, God bless him, Solomon had unloaded the truck by himself. He didn't want anything to go to waste. To me, that was mind-blowing—this little, old man doing all of that work by himself. Only Albert could convince him into letting me take the stuff to the dump.

As a window trimmer, I traveled a lot with Albert, whom I called Mr. B. One day, Mr. B took me to New York to see how they trimmed windows in the big city. I remember he walked me so much that my feet swelled. I couldn't get shoes on, so he bought me slippers, so I could go with him the next day.

What was it like working with Mr. B? Have you ever gone to the circus?

I just adored him.

Of course, some days we fought. One day, I worked all night on a window display, and he walked in the next morning and said, "I don't like it."

I said, "I don't care."

He just looked at me and laughed. That was our relationship. At the core of his creativity, Mr. B was a child who loved to play, and I was a puppy who sometimes barked back.

Another night, I had my two-year-old with me. I was divorced, working nights, and so she came along to work. That night, Mr. B saw her in the window and said, "Who are you?"

Of course, the two of them played for a while. Then he went down to the kitchen and got her a banana and a cookie, so she would have something to eat while I trimmed. I thought that was such a kindness.

One day, I was loading my toolbox into the car when I looked back and saw that the 9th street store was on fire. I had just finished the window display. The opening to the store windows were very small slots that you had to slide into, so I can only imagine what would have happened if I was still in the window when the fire started.

photo courtesy of Reading Eagle Company

Randy Reilly

My father picked me up from school and said, "Boscov's is on fire." We drove into town. All of Northeast Reading was there. The scene was crowded. Chaotic. The smoke was so thick we thought the house across the street was on fire. My God...I remember that store...the sloped floor...the shoe x-ray machine where kids would see their size shoe. You almost had to walk sideways between the aisles because there was so much merchandise. We were told it was an incinerator off of the receiving dock that did it, and that the firefighters had a hard time controlling the flames because of the building's metal frontage. That store was a landmark in Reading. Everyone in Northeast Reading used to shop there.

photo courtesy of Reading Eagle Company

Vivian Stephenson

I was the cashier in Sporting Goods the night that the old West store caught fire. It was the second store to catch fire within a year—first 9th and Pike, and then West. A stockman put a box too close to the furnace. The store manager announced that everyone should evacuate right away.

That same night was the grand opening for the new Boscov's East. This would have been November 1967. Albert and his father Solomon rushed over from the store opening to West. I remember the two of them just standing there, as their second store in a year went up in flames.

I remember when the fire first started, customers fled with their Boscov baskets of merchandise. During the Depression, when people were cash-strapped, Solomon gave them shoes for free. He told them, "Come back when you can pay. It's fine." A few years later, those customers returned and paid for their shoes. The same thing happened after the West Store fire. The people who ran out of the building with baskets of merchandise showed up at either the East or North store to pay for everything.

Of course, all of the coworkers felt awful about the fire, so we got together, and everyone donated a dollar to pay for a full-page ad in the newspaper, thanking Solomon, Albert, Ed, and the family for the stores and our jobs. It was our way of showing appreciation. The family showed its appreciation by reopening West the next year.

After the fire, everyone who worked at the West store came to East.

One day, Albert's executive assistant, Gerry Floto, needed help in the office, so I came down to help her. Well, that was forty-eight years ago. I've been Albert's executive assistant ever since, until he passed.

When I first started, his father Solomon would come in every day with cooked carrots and honey on rye bread. He would go from desk to desk and office to office, feeding everyone. Solomon was such a sweet man.

I was on maternity leave with my son when Solomon passed.

That would have been in August 1969.

The day Poppy passed away, we were on our way home from a family vacation in Beach Haven, New Jersey. We stopped for dinner at a restaurant along the way.

While we were eating, Poppy said he was having trouble breathing. We called an ambulance. I was eight years old. My sisters, Ellen and Meg, were six and three. We were all scared. Ellen remembers Poppy, in the middle of a heart attack, assuring her that he would be okay—that everything was all right.

When the ambulance arrived, Aunt Shirley Holzman and her family followed in one car while our family followed in another, zooming behind the ambulance. We were shocked to learn Poppy died on the way to the hospital. I remember the doctors offering my dad and Aunt Shirley tranquilizers, perhaps a standard practice of the time, to handle shock. Dad declined. I remember that and hugging my father, and that we both cried while holding each other.

Vivian Stephenson

Because I was on maternity leave with my son, I wasn't at the store the days following Solomon's death. But I heard Albert took four days off before returning to work. Even in his later years, whenever Albert talked about his father, he always got teary-eyed. He loved Solomon very much. I think Solomon was a role model for Albert, in life, for how to treat everyone with kindness, humility, and respect.

In business, Albert looked up a lot to a man named Max Hess. Max was a Jewish-German immigrant, who owned a department store in Allentown, Pennsylvania with his brother. A lot of the promotions that Albert came up with were inspired by Hess promotions. But so many promotions were pure Boscov's. When the *Reading Eagle* went on strike, Albert got the Boscov advertising and PR teams together to form *The Boscov Bugle*, a morning paper that even had its own advice column: "Dear Albie."

For Christmas and Easter, he hired Santa and the Easter Bunny to respectively parachute and fly in on a helicopter. One year, Santa opened his chute too late and broke his leg!

And, of course, there is "Did You Boscov Today," which is by far the most successful Boscov promotion of all time. It's been running for forty-eight years and counting.

Every day, Albert recorded memos, and I wrote them up word-for-word to send along to the buyers. Some days, I had four Dictaphone tapes to transcribe. But with all the promotions, there was always an excitement around the store. I never thought, "I hate to go to work today," because every day was different.

Albie's work philosophy was, "retail is recreation," and that was the key to his promotions' success. He made shopping fun. One time when he was in his twenties, he bought a whole bunch of miniature turtles. Any kid who came into the store on a Saturday with their parent got a turtle for free.

As Albie handed out the turtles, he said, "You do have turtle food at home, right?" Not many people did. For a quarter, he sold them turtle food, and that quarter covered his expenses. He had already broken even.

"Now," he said, "bring your turtles in next Saturday for the turtle races."

All of the neighborhood showed up at the store on consecutive Saturdays. The kids raced their turtles. The parents shopped, and I think Albie came out thinking that was a pretty good idea and started coming up with other promotions to get people excited about the store.

I remember once Roy Rogers' horse was in town. He arranged for the horse to appear at the 9th and Pike street store. Roy Rogers' horse might have been Boscov's first celebrity guest.

I remember calling up Albie and asking, "Is the horse there yet?"

Albie said, "Is he? He just peed all over the floor." He hung up and ran off to mop up.

One of Albie's wackiest promotions was when the Schultz family took over Boscov's. In the newspaper, Albie published an article saying, "There is no truth to the rumor that Boscov's is being sold."

There was no rumor (at least, not until he started it).

In the next day's paper, he wrote, "The Schultz family has said that they could do a better job running the store than the Boscov family, so we've decided to give them a chance at running the store."

For two weeks, Albie put the Schultz family in charge. Of course, he had made up the Schultzes. They supposedly were a hillbilly family from outside of Denver, but really all of Boscov's coworkers, buyers, and Albert's children dressed up in their farmer's best and became Schultzes by applying a black mole to their nose. Signs hung outside the front of the store that said "Schultz" instead of "Boscov." Hay littered the entrance, and corn dogs or some other carnival fare was served.

There were crazy specials, too. If your name was Schultz, you got a discount. At the end of the day, the customers got to vote on who they liked running the store more: the Schultz family or the Boscov

did you Schultz today

2 3 4 5

SCHULTZ 16 TIMES AND WIN A SCHULTZ PICNIC!

Schultz

EAST

16 15 14 13 12 11 10 9 8 7 6

family. After two weeks of Schultz sales, Albie published one last article in the paper announcing that the Boscov family won and the Schulz family was returning to wherever they were from in rural Denver. That was one of his best (and craziest) promotions.

Tammy Mitgang

I don't know what Albert's obsession was with chimps. But he loved Zippy. Zippy the Chimp was a roller-skating chimpanzee and one of our main attractions at Boscov's store openings. This was back in the late eighties. You most likely wouldn't do it today due to animal rights legislation.

What you may not know about performing chimps is that they are usually babies, so when you sat with them backstage, it was like sitting with a toddler. Zippy would look at books, or we would take him to the Greenery and he'd eat bananas, and all the customers at lunch loved it.

I can't say it enough. Nobody loved Zippy more than Albert. He was fascinated by him. As soon as Zippy entered the building, Albert was everywhere, singing, dancing, doing his shtick.

One store opening, Zippy was sick and couldn't come in.

I worked in PR under Mary Ann Chelius, so I was there when Albert realized that we wouldn't be able to book his favorite roller-skating chimpanzee.

He was exasperated, "We can't have a store opening without Zippy!"

He became obsessed with finding a replacement.

Every day, he called Mary Ann, "Did you find me a chimp?"

The next day: "Mary Ann, did you find me a chimp?"

Mary Ann finally found him a retired Zippy, who hadn't worked in years.

Albert said, "As long he can roller skate, it'll be fine. Trust me."

The day of the store opening came, and Mary Ann called me and said, "You better get over here. Zippy just got here." She did not sound happy. I hurried over to the auditorium, where the roller-skating performance was about to begin.

I could hear Mary Ann backstage. I went around the corner, and it was dark, and then there was this movement. For a second, I thought maybe it was the chimpanzee's handler.

No, Zippy the chimp was as tall as me. Up to that point, Mary Ann and I had never realized that we had been working with a baby chimpanzee. Full-grown, Zippy was over five feet tall, and chimps do not get cuter as they get older. They get kind of ugly-looking, and retired Zippy was this massive thing. We didn't know what to do, so we called Albert.

Albert came down and sized up the chimp, who was the same height as Albert. Albert turned to the chimp's handler, this old carny type who reeked of alcohol, and asked, "Can Zippy skate?" That's all Albert cared about! Whether Zippy could skate.

The man nodded.

Albert was satisfied. He left. That left me and Mary Ann, like, "Uhhh, we can't let that thing go out there."

Mary Ann said, "Why don't we see how the first show goes? It'll be fine, right?"

For the first show, this huge, not-cute chimp came lumbering out, in skates. Parents were terrified; the kids, speechless.

The next day, we were in the PR office when the phone rang.

Mary Ann listened. She said, "Uh huh... We'll be right over."

She hung up, then turned to me and said, "That was the fire department. There's a chimpanzee hanging out of the hotel balcony."

The handler and his full-grown chimpanzee had gotten a hotel room, and apparently he had gone out to drink and locked the chimpanzee in.

By the time we arrived, Zippy had destroyed the room, peeled the wallpaper off the walls, ripped the toilet from the floor, completely trashed the place, and now was hanging off of the hotel balcony.

The police and fire department were there. Spectators were looking up. We didn't know what to do, so we called Albert.

He said, "I guess we have to pay for the damages."

You guess?!!

Disappointed, he added, "And I guess we should send him home."

We never hired that handler or retired Zippy ever again. The good news is that our usual Zippy was ready for the next store opening, and I think that made Albert very happy.

Debby Wire

I was included in the promotion with Sofia Loren for her signature fragrance from Coty. The evening before the promotion, there was a cocktail party. Mr. Boscov and Sofia were onstage, chatting about her boys and a white rabbit he gifted her. At one point in the conversation, Sofia said, "You're the funniest little man I have ever met."

Without skipping a beat, Mr. B said, "But I'm tall when I stand on my money!" The comment was not a normal response from him to talk about his money, but it was just so spontaneous and unexpected that it was funny. It got a good laugh.

Barry Shaak

In 1972, I was a twenty-five-year-old kid. The boss (as I called Mr. B) gave me an opportunity. He asked if I wanted to be an assistant store manager.

I said, "Yes—what's an assistant store manager do?"

He said, "I'm still figuring that one out. It's a new position. Why don't I put you on store planning until the Lebanon store opens—

that way you'll be with me."

That's how I ended up working on store planning with him for the Lebanon store. We worked 24/7 for six months. The boss worked during the day with the vendors. At night, we did planning.

It was me, the boss, and two other characters. When you walk into a Boscov's that was built in the 1970s, you see wall mirrors everywhere and chandeliers. That was the work of Don Helms, who was the head of visual merchandise, and then there was Jerry Miller, who was a freelance designer. He came up with all of the store's color patterns. Jerry's favorite color was mauve, so everything in the store was done up in mauve from the carpets to the drapes.

Another eccentricity of Jerry's was that he would only leave New York City if the boss rented us a cabin for the summer in Bindenwood. The only way the four of us ever got work done was in that cabin.

One night in the cabin, the boss was marking up the store's floor plans with his red flair pen. While the boss worked, Jerry retrieved a hidden bottle of vodka, which he proceeded to dance with and wave about behind the boss's back. The boss, none the wiser, kept working. Jerry proceeded to spike everyone's iced teas, except for Mr. B's. The boss didn't drink.

While Mr. B. worked, the rest of us enjoyed Jerry's iced tea.

Then the boss went to pick up his own glass of iced tea, but it was empty, so he grabbed my glass and took a big, big gulp and slammed it down on the table.

The boss could swear like a sailor. The clean version of what he said is, "What the heck are you drinking, you gosh-darn drunks?"

Don had come from a wedding, so by this point in the evening, his mouth was so thick, tongue so numb, he couldn't talk. Our fun wasn't always like that.

On Sundays, we didn't always go to church; the four of us walked the store's construction site. Jerry liked to start water battles. We filled cups with water from the cooler and soaked each other. One time the boss got Jerry good! Jerry went to get him back. I saw Jerry coming, so I stepped in front of the boss—boom! I sacrificed myself for him.

Ever since, I had his loyalty. The boss would do anything for you once you had his loyalty. He gave me, a kid from a single-parent home, an opportunity to develop and learn, not only within retail, but also through his compassion, both as a person and as a man. I may have called him "boss," but he was a father to me.

Jim Boscov

Albert's father Solomon, who was my grandfather, traded in his 1955 Desoto for a used 1946 Ford Falcon. The Falcon had a three-speed manual transmission, no radio, and no heater. My grandmother Ethel was frustrated he got it.

She said, "Solomon, we have enough money now. You can afford a new car, and you come home with this old, used one?"

She refused to ride in it. For family get-togethers, my father or I would pick her up while my grandfather would take the Falcon. He died in 1969. But the car remained with the store for years and became a symbol of his humility. The buyers would take up a collection to get it a new transmission or new seats—whatever was needed to keep it running.

Albert was an infamously bad driver. His vehicle of choice was a wood-paneled station wagon that now sits in the back of the East store, where the Falcon used to be.

The "woodie" is still in use. Coworkers take it to run errands. Somewhere in my office, I have a report that says the wagon now has three or four hundred thousand miles on it. The goal is to keep it running as long as possible as a symbol of my grandfather's humility and, now, as a symbol of Albert's as well.

humility is a wood paneled station wagon

Dieter Czerny

When we were trying to get financing for the Doubletree Hotel, Albert drove once to meet with a bank. I was in the passenger seat. He drove reasonably well for a few feet, and then his advertising gene kicked in.

He asked me to find a particular page on the floor under my seat. His car was always full of ads—ads in Boscov's hand-baskets (his version of a briefcase) and, yes, ads on the floor, too.

I retrieved them.

He then received a phone call on his cell phone. He already had the newspaper ads pinned to the steering wheel.

Now I was holding a phone to his ear while he talked to a buyer. He then wished to speak with Vivian while the buyer was on the line.

I took out my cell phone and dialed Vivian.

Now I was holding two phones to his ear while he's doing ads. With him properly distracted, cars began honking.

I think the noises were his guideposts. When he heard a horn to his left, he drifted right. When a car beeped on his right, he veered left.

After this adventure, whenever we hit the road, of course I drove!

Albert wasn't fazed. He was still engrossed in his advertising pages, while safely ensconced in the passenger seat.

Once Albert and I were going over ads. We were in the back of the car, and Albert had a question about them for the fellow who was driving, so he took his pad of newspaper-sized proofs and stuck them in front of the guy's face. Of course, the fellow driving pushed the pad away so we wouldn't crash. Albert never gave it a second thought, never realized that he blocked the guy's view of the road. It didn't matter where we were going, or if we were going by car, bus, or plane. Traveling with Albert was a constant going-over of what we saw and what products we liked.

His mind never stopped. He was distracted while focused, which is why if you ask someone about the first time Albert drove them, you'll hear a lot of people say, "First time and last."

I have worked for Boscov's Travel for 43 years. When I first started, we had a large group going from Reading to Disney World. Their flight out of Philadelphia was scheduled to leave at 9 a.m. At the last minute, the charter company changed the flight to 6 a.m.

Mr. Boscov said, "Pat, we have to do something for all these people who've been inconvenienced. How many buses are leaving for Philadelphia?"

I said, "Three buses."

"I'll arrange with McDonald's to get everyone breakfast. Will you be seeing them off?"

"Yes, Mr. Boscov, but McDonald's won't be open." This was in 1974, and McDonald's wasn't yet 24 hours.

He said, "It's a big order. They'll take it. Your job is to get everyone organized in the parking lot and then onto their buses."

The buses were scheduled to leave at 3:30 am.

At three am, I'm standing in the middle of a parking lot. Now you have to remember that this is before cell phones. There was no way to call him, and there I was waiting, with everyone on the buses, and Mr. Boscov wasn't there.

I thought, "Oh no, what am I going to do?"

The bus driver came to me and said, "Look, little girlie," which I didn't appreciate. Even then, I was a feminist, but back then people got away with talking like that, so the bus driver said to me, "Look, little girlie, we have to let these buses go or these people are going to miss their flight."

"Okay. But I'm waiting for Mr. Boscov."

"Sorry, we've got to go."

They left. I was alone in the dark parking lot. My car was the only one left in the lot. I started walking to it when Mr. Boscov flew into the lot in his father's Ford Falcon. This was before he had his wood-paneled station wagon, so he was in Solomon's car and driving like a wild man. I could see the stuff flying around in the back of the car, and he said, "Pat, where are the buses?"

I said, "Mr. B, I'm sorry, I had to let them go."

"How long ago?"

"Eight... ten minutes ago."

"Get in the car. We'll get them."

"We're going to catch the buses?"

"We're going to catch the buses."

Now, I had never driven with Mr. B before. I believe only by God's grace did he ever get around. We were going down 422 in this rickety little car at about eighty miles an hour.

There! We could see the buses. They were going over the hills, and he said, "Don't worry"—as he put the pedal to the floor—"we'll catch them."

So now we're going down 422 at ninety miles per hour. He got in the left lane, running tandem with the three buses, beeped his horn at them, and said, "They're not stopping, Pat."

I said, "I don't think they will."

"Hang your head out the window and—"

"What?"

"Wave them down."

Who am I to say no?

I was waving at the buses, with my head hanging out the window, and the bus driver looked at me, and he probably thought I was a crazy woman at this point. The buses didn't stop.

Mr. Boscov said, "Don't worry. I'll stop the buses!"

"You—what?"

He pulled in front of them and went sideways on 422. I'll say that again. We were going sideways on 422 at four in the morning, and three buses filled with people slammed on the brakes. You could see over one hundred people getting whiplash. On 422, the Falcon was horizontal. The three buses were parked.

Mr. B got out of the car. He got on the bus, and he said, "Good morning, I'm Al Boscov."

Nobody knew who he was, but he charmed every one of them. He even charmed the bus driver. He went up and down the aisle, handing out breakfast sandwiches and thanking everyone.

When it was over, he told me, "I'm sorry I was late. McDonald's didn't have the order ready, but we delivered on our customer promise. That's what matters—and that we made friends."

You'd think the ride back would be easier. Going back he was going 80 miles an hour. Oh my, it was absolutely wonderful.

Ellen Boscov

One of the games Dad liked to play with us was about a bunny named Billy. Billy Bunny was a police bunny. Now I'm told by my older sister Ruth that Dad played "Billy Bunny" with us while seated in an armchair. But because Dad was such a good storyteller, I remember the game taking place in an actual car. It all seemed so real. Dad would be driving...a little too fast.

All of a sudden, WOO-WOO! Billy Bunny was after him. In real life, Billy Bunny was a stuffed animal, but in the game, Billy Bunny was an authority figure.

He would tell Dad, "HEY YOU, you're driving too fast. Now I got to give you a ticket."

We three girls would beg, "No, no. Don't give him a ticket. Please."

"Daddy just made a mistake."

"Give him a break."

I can't remember if we ever talked Billy Bunny out of giving him a ticket. But in Dad's games and in all of his stories, he was a trickster who foiled the big mean authority figure, and we'd stick up for him because he really was just one of us kids. People sometimes talk about Dad, the retail giant... this big man. I don't think he ever thought of himself that way. In lots of his stories and in life, I think he really was just a little guy, trying to help a lot of other little guys.

Josh Aichenbaum

My mom found a journal entry of hers from August 27, 2000. She wrote:

Tomorrow, my dad is being honored. A highway is being named after him. When I asked him about it, he said it's not a big deal, it's really nothing. They're just putting up a few signs that say, 'For your own safety, stay off the road when Al Boscov is driving.'

If you are on 422 in Exeter Township, from Mount Penn to Shelbourne Road, you will come upon signs that say, "Albert Boscov Commemorative Highway. "

Slow down to the speed limit, drive safely, or you may just see Billy Bunny speeding out of his cut-out to give you a ticket.

Albert used to come into New York every week and ask me, "What's new? What's exciting?"

He was always looking for deals. At the time, I was with Merchant Buying Syndicate. I would get him deals, and he always loved them. We had a division that went on trips overseas, so one time, we took Albert and a whole group on a buying trip through Asia: to Hong Kong, Korea, Taiwan, and Japan.

Before the trip, I went to a hypnotherapist because I was always trying to lose weight. The hypnotherapist recorded a tape for me. If I listened to it every day, it was supposed to help me quit eating junk food. Of course, the tape didn't work—not even close.

The group was on a bullet train in Asia. Albert went up to a vendor who was carrying a basket of ice cream and said, "How many are in there?"

She said, "Fifty or sixty..."

He said, "I'll buy all of them, and I want the basket, too."

Albert put the rope around his neck, and he handed out ice cream to everyone on the trip, up and down the aisle. Wherever Albert went, he always ended up being the leader of the group. Everybody loved him because he was so much fun.

On that trip, Albert and I ate our way through Asia. The more we ate, the better friends we became. In the morning, it was lox omelets. For lunch, he loved shrimp. One day, we ordered a big bowl of them. The shrimp came live. The server doused them with oil and cooked them in front of us. By the end of the trip, Albert and I had each gained ten pounds. I have a picture of him laughing on the plane ride home, as he listened to my failure of a diet tape.

To me, one of the greatest joys of my life was my relationship with Albert. He was my best friend and the most amazing person. We didn't see each other much, with me in New York, but we talked to each other regularly, and he'd give me advice and talk me through difficult times. There was this great love and bond between us.

Stefanie Brocchi

My dad was best friends with Albert. They did business together and did their best to avoid dieting together. Albert always knew what motivated people. I remember when my dad got a new job, his coworkers initially weren't taking to him. He went to Albert for advice. Albert told him, "Buy them bagels one day. The best way to your heart is through your stomach."

My dad took his advice. All of a sudden, my dad had all kinds of new relationships at work. Albert was a great mentor and friend to my father.

When I was a little kid, we would go to Pennsylvania. Albert would take my sister and me into the store, and he'd hide with us under the coat rack and tell us stories, or he would take us to the

a full stomach is a happy person

candy department to scoop out chocolates. Here he was running a whole company, but he still took the time out of his day to be kids with us.

David Hick

I've been working at Boscov's since I was a kid in Wilkes-Barre, PA. When I graduated from college, I interviewed to enter the Boscov executive training program. My final interview was with Mr. Boscov; his sister Shirley Holtzman, who ran the human resources department; and Ed Lakin. I was so nervous. Mr. Boscov could sense it. He asked me if I wanted a piece of cheesecake. He stopped the interview and we all ate cheesecake. The rest of my interview was very relaxed and fun. I'll never forget how he put my mind at ease.

Corrine King

It was VIP day, and Mr. Boscov was there. If you're not familiar with VIP, vendors come to the store to show off their merchandise: usually housewares, small appliances, and candy. At morning meeting, we were told the candy was for customers only.

While we worked, Patty Yager and I kept eying it.

I said, "Patty, we're not allowed to have any, remember?"

Mr. Boscov heard us. He turned around and said, "Who says

you can't?"

I said, "In morning meeting, they said customers only."

"You know what? I'm the boss."

He fetched us the tray and told us to take "all you want."

Alice Sweeney

When you worked with Mr. B on ads, you worked long hours, late into the night. We'd be in the conference room, with all the ads for the week on the table. All of a sudden, he'd say, "Hold on, gang. I'll be right back."

He'd come back with a box of Chief Cruchies or ice cream to get everyone through the night. Sometimes, if the cafeteria was closed, the advertising team would do what he called "thieving." Everyone and Mr. B would go behind where they served the food, and he'd open all the refrigerators.

Of course, the first thing he'd show us was the desserts. He was quite the showman.

He would hold up options and say, "Here we have a lovely cherry pie. Do I have any takers? We also have olives and, uh, a beautiful, open-faced tuna sandwich!"

The funniest part was whenever we'd "thieve," he'd rat himself out. He would take out his tape recorder and record what he had "stolen" so someone would know to charge him for the food. He'd say, "Vivian, tonight, I took two ice cream bars—and a tuna sandwich."

Danielle Ashbridge

Back in August 2016, Mr. B had a bus trip planned to our Granite Run store. We wanted to do something special for him, so we ordered a big cake with a picture of him on it wearing a hard hat since our location was then a construction zone. Our visual manager Laura and I ran around, getting everything ready, so we could present him with the cake.

When he finally made it around to see the cake, he was so happy and touched. The funny part was that he thought the picture of him was supposed to be Donald Trump, which made everyone laugh.

He was so excited, he started singing and wanted to serve the cake to all of the customers and workers. It was such a special moment to be there with him, helping serve cake and listening to him sing. Of course, he enjoyed a slice of cake for himself as well.

He really was in all his glory. That moment really showed me how much he was there to serve his coworkers and customers.

Pat DeAngelis

I think it was 1963. I was in a band called The Jesters, and we were hired to play for the Boscov's employees' summer picnic. During one of our breaks, Mr. Boscov and four of his top managers or buyers went onstage and sat on chairs for all to see. The store had an emcee to conduct the festivities. The M.C. put salon capes over Al and all of the other "big guys" of "this great store" and called up onstage a handful of employees. The employees were supposed to build ice cream sundaes on top of the heads of these executives.

To put the employees at ease, so they wouldn't have second thoughts or "chicken out," (because the executives were their bosses), some pretty nice prizes were awarded to the contestant who made the best sundae on the head of these good sports. Needless to say, the show was hilarious and probably yielded the best employee relations you could ever hope for. I did then and have always respected Al Boscov. As big a personality as he was, he didn't mind being laughed at as long as his employees had a great time!

Bethann Wagner

My office was always right across the hall from Mr. B's office on the advertising side, but until these last few years, he could never remember my name. He simply knew me as Mary Beth, Anne, "honey," or the little girl in the office next to Ed's. But whatever name he used, Vivian and I always knew he was looking for me!

When I first started at Boscov's, I always had peppermint patties in a jar on my desk. One morning I came in, and there were no peppermint patties in the jar, but there was a five-dollar bill.

Days passed. My peppermint patties would disappear. When the jar was empty, I would find dollar bills in it instead. Mr. B would take peppermint patties out during the day, but it took me a few weeks to realize he was the one leaving the money. One day when he took the last peppermint patty out of the jar, he wanted to give me a dollar for it. I told him "No, no I am fine." It was then that I realized he was leaving the money so the jar would keep refilling!

You know now that he is gone, it's like—so quiet. I always used to hear him yelling, "Vivian! Vivian! Can you get so-and-so on the line?" It wasn't loud noise, but it was always there in the background —his singing, talking, having fun. I really miss him.

Jeff Mitgang

My first trip into the market with Albert was July 35 years ago. We were going to the old New York coliseum, and we were going to meet all the executives from Vanity Fair. Now Vanity Fair was a very rigid, corporate structure. Albert took our whole entourage from sportswear and men's, and he paraded us in. Behind a table stood *boom boom boom* six Vanity Fair men in a row, all in pinstripe suits, white shirts, and wingtip shoes—all cut from the same mold. Now Albert got on his hands and knees, and he crawled under the table to shake the president's hand.

Those six men didn't know what hit them.

Now, hold it. This was clever. Albert broke the ice. From then on, he had them in the palm of his hand. He took out his notebook and expounded all of these figures and opportunities, and this and that, turning the pages, except every page was blank. I'm pretty sure he had a photographic memory. We sure had a great meeting.

People wanted to produce for Albert. I wouldn't call it work. It was always a challenge. He gave you parameters to work with, but it was always, "Do a great job! Jeff, do an honest job."

When we were opening the Albany store, the first two days were lackluster. Sales were only okay, so the whole team was a little down.

Then Sunday came, and the floodgates opened. The only outside entrance went straight into gifts, and domestics was behind that.

For some reason, that market was fixated on domestics. Within an hour of opening, it literally looked like a swarm of locusts had gone through the department. Mr. B took the whole management team up to the stockroom and proceeded to climb up the shelving and throw down any comforter he could get his hands on. We put them on a lift and took them to the floor. We filled the bins, and then lined up the comforters in front of all the

curtain displays. He was singing and joking the whole time. I knew he worked constantly, but it's the only time I saw the owner of a company climb up stockroom shelving to get merchandise.

This of course repeated itself with every classification in the department—sheets, towels, pillows, table linens. We couldn't get out of domestics. Then he started joking with me, calling me Wayne and telling everyone that "Wayne just loves domestics!" This scenario repeated itself throughout the remainder of November and December, because he was there with us every Saturday.

It doesn't sound like much, but the fact that he had a running joke with me calling me Wayne and telling everyone how much I loved domestics made me feel that he valued me. From that day on, I would have done anything he asked me to do. He knew how to instill loyalty in people.

Ed McKeaney

Back in the early days of the company, Mr. Lakin and Mr. Boscov would review our performance yearly. Because they worked so many hours, you never knew when your review would happen. One year my review actually started at 3 a.m. I was in my late twenties, and I was hoping for a raise. Albert and I were on one side of Mr. Lakin's desk, and Mr. Lakin was on the other. We were going back and forth for a while...I don't know how long. Finally we got to the end of my review.

Mr. Boscov said, "Well, Ed, we've decided your raise is going to be—" and he fell asleep. He was out cold and was snoring very loudly. I looked from him to Mr. Lakin, who just shrugged because he didn't know what to do either. Mr. Lakin and I started talking when suddenly Al woke up and shouted, "Twenty dollars a week!"

Somehow, he never missed a beat.

Lisa Moore

One night, Mr. B was doing a jewelry inventory all by himself. He sat down with the inventory. But he was so tired that he fell asleep. Nobody knew that he was still at the store, so they all locked up and left. When he woke up, the lights were off, and no one was around. He stood up and set off every alarm in the store!

The police rushed to the scene, and there he was, just waving to the cops from the inside.

Brian Foley

It was the day before a store opening in New Jersey. Mr. B loved to look at every item in the Gifts Department down to the individual forks and knives, so much so that soon it was 9:30 p.m. The person who was supposed to drive him back wanted to leave, but Mr. B wasn't ready. Since I worked in Gifts, the driver told me, "You take him back to the hotel." I said I certainly would.

When Mr. B was finally ready to go, we set off in my Pontiac Sedan. On the way, we talked about various things, not just business. Before I knew it, we had arrived outside the hotel lobby. My intent was to get out and open the door for him, but he didn't give me the chance. Instead, he began pulling on the handle—to no effect.

I said, "Mr. B, you have to unlock the door first. Press the button forward."

But he just kept pulling. I reached in front of him to unlock it, but he gave my hand a light smack and proceeded to pull.

I said, "Let me help, " but he insisted, "I got it," and kept pulling on the handle. I kept trying to unlock it, but I'd reach, and he'd slap away my hand, and I'd reach, and so on. It was like we were in a slapstick comedy routine.

Finally, I got out of the car and opened the door for him from the outside. He calmly got out, turned to me, and said very straight-faced, "Nice car, Brian, but you really need to get your locks fixed."

I giggled all the way home.

We were all exhausted. It was the night before the Plymouth Meeting Boscov's store opening, and we had all been working from very early in the morning until eleven o' clock at night. Albert chose three flights of stairs over waiting for the elevator.

Come the third flight, he couldn't make it up the last few steps, so he fell back into my arms, and I carried him the rest of the way like a tired baby.

What do you think he did?

Naturally, he stuck his thumb in his mouth and sucked his thumb. That happened in 1996. Around the same time, Strawbridge and Clothier closed its doors in Plymouth Meeting. Strawbridge and Clothier had a wonderful program: in essence, a charity day. Between fifty and sixty charities depended on that day for their annual fundraising.

So, I suggested to Albert we take up the slack and start a charity day of our own. That's how Friends Helping Friends got started. At first, it was just Plymouth Meeting, but the event proved so successful, the whole company joined in.

The gist of the program is that local charities fundraise by selling five-dollar tickets that grant entrance to Boscov's on a day in October when customers get twenty-five percent off.

For Albert to step in and run with the idea was monumental; it helped so many communities, but for Boscov's, it's also our best day of the year. The program is a win-win for everybody. But that's what happens when you can count on your friends for support.

I've been reflecting on my time before I was a manager at Boscov's. Every year, retailers meet in Las Vegas. I was the national sales manager with London Fog at the time, and I had 20,000 units to move on a closeout basis and an appointment with a Boscov's buyer.

I remember a buzz around our booth. Mr. Boscov had decided to sit in on the discussions. He sat quietly as the buyer and I set the program in place. After the meeting, my boss asked me whether I had moved the units. I replied I had, in a fair way for London Fog and Boscov's: a win-win deal.

He asked if I had the "paper?"

I said, "Yes. Not only did we book the order on a handshake, but more importantly we sealed the deal on a hug."

seal a deal
with a hug

Frank Strawbridge

My great-grandfather was Justus Clayton Strawbridge. In 1868, he opened a dry goods business with Isaac Hallowell Clothier, which is how Strawbridge & Clothier department stores got started. We were always friendly competitors with Boscov's. Boscov's was in Reading, PA, and we were based out of Philadelphia.

In 1994, when Wanamaker's went out of business, we took interest in a number of the Wanamaker stores. We didn't want all of them, so we approached Boscov's to see if they wanted to get together. Al wanted the Wanamaker store in Reading, and he wanted the Wanamaker store in King of Prussia.

It ended up being us, Federated, Boscov's, and a private developer that joined forces to bid on Woodward & Lothrop, which was Wanamaker's parent company. We were competing on the bid against Penney's and the May Company.

In June 1995, our group and Al's team took the train from Philadelphia to New York. We were going before a judge to put in our bid. On the train, while my team studied our financials, Al was in the same car as us; but while we talked six-figures, he wrote ads for undershirts at 4.99, or whatever the items and price were that day. In the end, Penney's and the May Company outbid us. Strawbridge and Clothier and Boscov's didn't get the stores. But I think that was typical of Al. He was always more focused on the customer, the ads, and business the next day than on expansion or making a major transaction. In that moment on that train, I got to appreciate the Al Boscov approach to business.

Jane M. Von Bergen

Philadelphia Inquirer, Daily News, and Philly.com

You might have needed hazard pay to sit across from Al Boscov during a meal.

That's because Boscov was a habitual multitasker, including talking, counting up sales figures, and going over marketing budgets, all while chewing, and yes, spewing.

Other than brushing off a soggy bagel crumb or two, it was what made Al Boscov a pleasure to cover—he acted like everybody else, except more energetic. Except more friendly. Except more funny.

In 1996, as a *Philadelphia Inquirer* business reporter covering retailing, I got a chance to tag along with Al on one of his bi-weekly bus trips to the stores. Two buses packed with merchandise buyers would head out from Reading and travel to a handful of stores clustered in a geographic area. The goal of the trip was to keep the buyers who selected the merchandise in touch with the store personnel who sold it.

The morning I went was an experience.

Everyone was on the bus, and Al was running late. I worried on his behalf, which was stupid, of course, since it was his company and the buses weren't going anywhere without him.

When he arrived he made sure I got my bagel and coffee and then he grabbed his bagel—whole, uncut, no spread, no napkin—and jammed it into his suit pocket. Beautiful.

Great detail for my story, but also for me personally; I felt so comfortable.

Business reporters meet a lot chief executives, and most of them are buttoned up and all too rehearsed. It might sound weird to say that I felt physically comfortable around Al, but I did. You could take your shoes off, or put your feet up. You could simply relax. Journalists don't relax. Besides, I knew the story would take care of itself. All I had to do was watch and write.

We got on the bus and Al parked himself in the back, jammed next to the toilet.

We saw everybody coming... and going.

Al pulled the bagel out of his pocket, detached the Post-it note, brushed off some lint, and took a big bite, chomping and chatting. Then he tossed the bagel back into his executive attaché case—a green plastic crate like the ones you get in the supermarket when you only have a few items to buy. The bagel promptly got buried under a notebook, a stack of computer printouts, and some old

photo courtesy of *The Citizens' Voice*

photo courtesy of *The Citizens' Voice*

advertising circulars.

I loved it. This man made a lot of points with me just by being himself and acting like a normal human being, although I guess most people don't eat bagels with lint. Personally, I like cream cheese.

At the start of the trip, he made his way to the front and, as the bus rolled away from Reading, rattled off sales stats—which stores were doing well, which weren't, what was selling, what wasn't.

Then he adjourned to the rear for his back-of-the-bus marketing meetings, one-on-one with various buyers. He pulled computer printouts out of the crate and scanned lists of prices and sales. He compared advertising circulars from the same week in the previous year with the sales results. What worked. What didn't. The buyers told him what they thought should be advertised.

Soon the bus swung into the parking lot of the first store—this one was in Norristown.

Inside the store, Boscov stopped to pull a box of stockings out of a display bin so the front of the package would show. He told the manager to consider unboxing a set of twin lamps on sale for $49.99 to sell them individually for $24.99. "They might sell better that way." So many great memories from that day:

I remember watching his nephew wince as Al ran down the up escalator. The nephew was halfway between worried that Al, then 67, would fall, and embarrassed, like a teenager regularly humiliated by an older relative.

I remember watching Al hopscotch on a Twister game that had been painted onto the floor in a children's department. By that time, I was tired. Al was not.

I remember watching Al hold the hand of the jewelry department manager, swinging her hand as he walked down the aisle with her, casual, comfortable, intimate, affectionate, not uptight and formal.

"Anything you need?" he asked her. She smiled and said no. He smiled and gave her hand an extra squeeze before letting go.

Over the years, I interviewed Al Boscov several times, having first met him in a Manhattan bankruptcy court when I was covering the breakup of the John Wanamaker chain and he was trying to buy some of the stores. The suits and the other execs were clearly uptight, but not Al Boscov, who stood in the hallway, joking around, ever friendly.

In Reading, Al Boscov didn't have a fancy office in the department store chain's (way) less-than-elegant headquarters tucked in the back of one of the stores. Truthfully, his digs, though comfortable, were a mess, the working quarters of someone actually working, with meetings held at a conference table that had clearly seen better days.

That's another reason I liked him. Many of the chief executives I visit have suspiciously clean desks. They make me nervous. But I liked Al's messiness. It seemed truthful and realistic and comfortable. Work is messy. That's just how it is.

I last interviewed Al in 2014 and I took my son, then 23, along to the interview, because I wanted him to meet an executive who didn't need a mission statement to have a mission and because I wanted him to see what real no-frills, kind-hearted leadership looked like. On that day, Al explained that he'd be working on Thanksgiving because the store employees were working and that all of them would have an excellent catered meal, served during their breaks.

Reporters should never harbor the illusion that they are friends with the people they cover, even people they like, even people who appear to like them. That being said, I'm so sorry I'll never be able to interview Al Boscov again.

I met Albert twenty-five years ago, as a vendor selling to Boscov's. I miss him every single day. He gave me a chance, and he believed in me. In 1993, I started a business with him and Ed Lakin called Tristar Products Inc.

Albert was always a huge cheerleader—not just for me, but for many of the Boscov employees and families. He would tell you, "Don't worry, everything will be all right," and then he would take on the responsibility to make sure that everything would be, without letting you know he was doing it. In the first two years of my business, I came to him twice, in need of Albert the cheerleader.

The first time, we had a product called glamor tail. It was a hair styling tool to give women quick and easy hair styles. In those days, we included a VHS tape with the product. Well, the video duplicating house slipped up. In the box with your hair styling tools, the duplicating house accidentally slipped in a video for how to deworm a cow. I thought Albert would terminate our relationship on the spot. I was so nervous to tell him. I thought he would yell and get mad, but when I told him what happened, he laughed so hard I actually thought he would choke. That was Albert, always laughing, giving you support, and being your biggest cheerleader.

That was the first year of the business.

The second year, we actually lost money. In business, when you don't have a great year, you get a little down on yourself.

I went to him, and I said, "Mr. B, I feel like a failure."

He looked me in the eye and said, "Son, you haven't failed. You fail when you quit. You just haven't succeeded yet."

The next year was our biggest year yet. We had a product called the ab roller, and it was huge hit for us. Twenty years later, that ab roller is still selling.

you haven't failed yet ; you just haven't succeeded

Erich Sheaffer

I'm a former Boscov's employee. I worked at East where Mr. Boscov had his office. My father, Dean Sheaffer, is the SVP of finance/credit at Boscov's, so growing up, I had a great deal of admiration for Mr. B.

My first week as an employee, I was still learning to use the register. I was in the men's department when a huge rush of customers came in, and I was all alone. Mr. B just happened to be checking out the floor at the time. Due to the layout of East, when you walk up from the basement where the executive offices are, the first thing you see is the men's department and my register. He saw me flustered, struggling, and generally in distress, and he came over, put his hand on my shoulder, and told me to take it slow and that everything would be all right. He talked to the customers in line to keep them happy while I fumbled with the register.

After the last customer, he told me that I did great. Because of my existing admiration and respect for him, it caused me a great sense of joy, pride, and a million other emotions all at once.

Bill Gallagher

I came to Boscov's as a buyer, and then I was promoted. I ended up being the senior VP for home furnishings, a position which took me all over the world. In the late eighties, I had a trip planned for the Far East. Albert told me, "I'm coming with you this time."

We went to Hong Kong, Taiwan, Korea, and Japan, in search of merchandise.

Wherever we traveled, for some reason, Albert and I ended up roommates, with a set of double beds.

One morning, I woke up, and I heard rummaging. I had several days of clothing in my bag, and there was Albert, searching through my clothes.

He said, "I under-packed—just need some underwear.""

He took my underwear and wore it. Later, I went into the

bathroom, and there he was brushing his teeth with my toothbrush.

That was my boss—that was Albert, all right. He never had the right things with him. But he always made sure anything he got involved in was done right.

I spent many, many hours with him shopping for merchandise. He never purchased an item out of convenience or because it was easy to do and be done with. He didn't take the first product presented to him. He was thorough because...if you're going to do something, you ought to do it right.

Jeff Mitang

First year I was with the store, we were on one of our weekly bus trips to New York to discover merchandise.

Albert hopped on the bus and said, "I have an announcement to make. Our January trip this year is to—Hawaii!"

Hawaii?!

I nearly pinched myself. I had jobs in which you're lucky to get your paycheck.

Each year, Albert took all of the buyers, vendors, merchandisers, and their families on a phenomenal trip to the Caribbean or somewhere else equally sunny; he did it because he expected a lot from you from Thanksgiving to Christmas. That was a difficult stretch with long hours. But he rewarded you for your hard work by taking you on a spectacular trip.

In Hawaii, one night we had a party that was MASH-themed

(because MASH was going off the air). For dinner, the entire back half of the hotel was set up like an army compound. Everybody wore scrubs. You walked through a mess line, carrying a tray as if you were in the army. But instead of slop, each station had steak or fish.

What a party!

I remember Ed Lakin flew in on a helicopter like the wounded and the alcohol came in syringe bottles.

Albert had a way of making hard work fun. Sure, every day wasn't a party. There were tough days. But everybody was in it together, and Albert was there with everyone fighting—or more likely, singing—in the trenches.

Rob and Yvonne Oppenheimer: The Boat Disaster Part I

One year our trip was to St. Thomas and we had to fly into St. John and then get to St. Thomas by either seaplane or boat. There were around three hundred of us on the trip and we could choose which way we wanted to go. About seventy-five of us chose the sightseeing boats. We set out around 3 p.m. on a beautiful afternoon with the blue Caribbean beneath us.

About an hour into the trip, we were in a squall and tossing badly. Turns out the captain and crew were inexperienced, lost, and their navigation and communication equipment had failed. We held onto the railings and watched numbly as our luggage slid from one side of the deck to the other.

Pat Clifton: The Boat Disaster Part 2

There were two decks to the boat, and we were on the top deck, so we had air. The people in front of me were eating bananas. Everybody else was throwing up. Ann Merkel was sitting, hunched over. Not moving. I thought to myself, "I know Annie's Jewish, but I bet she's saying her rosary."

The dress buyer Diane Jackson was sitting in front of me with her husband. They had their daughter on the trip, and she had just gotten a Barbie for Christmas. Sure enough, Barbie went into the deep. Barbie was the only one smart enough to abandon ship.

Mary Ann Chelius was on our boat, too. She was the head of Public Relations. When she saw the crew passing out life jackets, she stopped them because there clearly weren't enough to go around.

Mary Ann didn't want the situation to end up becoming, "Come on! Give me your life jacket! Give it here!"

Tammy Mitang: The Boat Disaster Part 3

The waves were all over the place, and the ferry was flat-bottomed, so it couldn't turn. We were in open water, and we had been out there for hours, and we were out there, and it was getting darker and rougher, and we were going nowhere. You lose all confidence in everything when you see the crew is sick.

Then the engine cut out. The lights, too. We lost power.

I was on the top deck with my husband.

I said, "Jeff, this isn't good. We're in the middle of a ship lane at night. They'll never see us." If we didn't get in, a ship would hit us. I remember having conversations with him, saying that I was so happy that our son wasn't with us.

Luckily, the storm calmed down enough, so the ship could get to shore.

The boat ride was supposed to be an hour. It ended up being six or seven. Everyone was drenched and shivering. Some couldn't walk because they were so sick. When we got off the boat, Albert was standing there, crying, inconsolable. He thought he lost everyone. His brother Joe and sister-in-law Shirley had been on the boat along with everyone else.

Through his tears, he announced, "Don't worry. I made sure they kept the buffet open." Food was his consolation. We were so sick, and he's yelling, "Don't worry, the buffet is open!"

Of course, the rest of the trip was wonderful.

Joan Rasmussen

I am a footwear vendor who worked with Boscov's for many years. Mr B was a wonderful person, who I greatly admired for many reasons.

True to form he was a gentleman, and a salesman to the end. I was fortunate to have known him. I am remembering how well he treated all his employees, vendors, customers, and everyone he came into contact with. Everyone loved him.

Mr. B was the type of retailer who you wanted to do things for because his heart and soul were in it. His enthusiasm was contagious.

Case in point, we are on the Boscov Punta Cana vendor's trip, and I am one of the lucky vendors who won. Mr. B and his family are staying in a room down the hall from me. I would get up very early every morning with my husband to reserve the chairs and towels for all of the Boscov footwear people.

One morning I am walking down the hall, and I hear Mr B whistling and singing "Zip-a-dee-doo-dah. There's a bluebird on my shoulder."

My husband and I say good morning to him and continue on our way to the pool. But I can't get the song or Mr. B singing it out of my mind. He was so happy!

In the early afternoon there are many footwear people in the pool. I relay the story to them. We start to sing, and before you know it, we are singing, "Zip-a-dee-doo-dah" over and over, and laughing like crazy (granted there were some firewater shots involved).

Walking by with his family, Mr. B overhears us. He is smiling, tapping his foot, and singing the song along with us. We all sing together. We are cheering and laughing, and it is quite a special moment.

One we will never forget.

Later at the awards dinner, Mr. B announces everyone has to stand up and sing the national anthem. We all stand with our hands on our hearts. But on-screen is "Zip-a-dee-doo-dah" with a ball bouncing on the words. We all laugh and sing along again. It is a special moment for everyone in the room.

That was so like him. He saw a common way to bring us all together and create a memory, just like he did for his customers. We all bonded over that, and we still all talk about it. He had a way about him. His enthusiasm was contagious. His outlook was always "My oh my what a wonderful day, plenty of sunshine headed our way…"

He will be missed by everyone. He was unique. They don't make them like him anymore. They broke the mold the day he was born.

Rest in peace, Albert. Please look over us as you do. We will need you to make sure we all walk the straight and narrow and follow your example.

It is we who are proud of you and everything you represent. You will be the bluebird who will watch over us now.

I've been working here twenty years, currently in fine jewelry, and my husband was a buyer. We went on a lot of wonderful store trips, once to Porta de Varta, and to Arizona three times. The two of us were in Rio de Janeiro, swimming, when all of a sudden Mr. Boscov jumped into the pool and grabbed our hands. He sang, "Ring around the rosie, pockets full of posie, ashes, ashes..."

And we all fell down! We swam and talked. That summed up exactly who he was.

begin every day with a song

Lori Abramowitz Campisano

Every Wednesday, Boscov buyers go to New York to find new merchandise. To be honest, sometimes riding on the bus on those dark, cold Wednesday mornings was pretty tough, but every time

I would see Mr. B riding along, too, offering us bananas with a huge "good morning" smile (often while singing), I would think to myself, "If he can still do this at his age, so can I."

Todd Gimbi-German

Kurt and I met through Boscov's in 1990 in the coal regions of Pennsylvania. When Pennsylvania made gay marriage legal in 2014, Kurt and I decided we'd go in, sign the papers, and not make a big deal of it. We had been together for more than twenty years. We showed up at the downtown Reading courthouse, thinking there would be lines going around the block and everyone would be excited to finally get married, but we wound up being the only people there. Our photo ended up on the cover of the *Reading Eagle*.

Albert was so happy for us. He came in the next morning and put a stack of newspapers on my desk. He was so ecstatic that he had gone around, collecting the paper. I always thought it was so cool that he was so loving and accepting of everyone, no matter who they were. He was such a loving person. He'd call me *cutiepie* and hold my hand while we walked the sales floor.

Unfortunately, a couple of years ago, I became seriously ill. I wound up in the hospital from March to June.

Mr. B came in to see me. He sat next to me, and he held my hand for hours. Literally for hours he held my hand and talked to me about me about how he once had a heart condition but overcame it. For the first time in our relationship, he was no longer my boss or my idol. He became a real person, who had taken the time out of his busy schedule to be with me.

When I came back to work, he worried about me every day.

He kept asking, "How are you feeling? Are you working too hard? If you're working too hard— "

I said, "No, no, I've got to work." I cared so much about my job.

I'm now fabulous and healthy, thankfully. But I miss him every day. Sometimes I feel lost without him, with all these memories...

I think about what he would want me to do, what he wants for his company, and what he's done for everyone.

I owe him everything—my life and my relationship.

I think he'd want everyone to be happy, so every day I hold the same morning huddle that I've always done. He used to love it.

Before the store opens, all of the East coworkers gather together, and we sing, and we dance to begin the day.

Ruth Boscov Aichenbaum

My first memory of my dad working his magic to make a difference in the world was when I was seven years old and he held a Heritage Festival for the Black Community of Berks County.

As a child the festival was exciting. My sisters and I ate delicious food, listened to great jazz and blues, and got to know the wonderful drummer Babatunde Olatunji, who was originally from Nigeria. Even though I was just seven, I was aware that the festival was more than just fun; the festival was doing important work. I noticed the signs all around the store which read *Knowing is Understanding.* From Dad's explanation, I understood that this festival was about educating our community and fighting prejudice.

It wasn't until I was an adult and I spoke to him about this festival that I fully appreciated how brilliant and impactful it was.

I learned that Dad came up with the idea for the festival because he was concerned with the unequal treatment and lack of career opportunities for blacks in the North.

He wanted our local black community to be the actual organizers of the festival so that they could have the pride of running it, so he went to meetings of black organizations and spoke to them about the idea of holding a festival in his stores (in 1968 there were only two Boscov's— both in Reading).

From those meetings people stepped forward to be the leaders of the festival. Together with these leaders, he then started having luncheons with white businessmen in Reading to get their support for the festival and their agreement to run ads stating that they were an equal opportunity employer.

He also reached out to businesses and citizens to start college scholarships so that any member of the black community could go to college free on the condition that they would then return to Reading to enrich our community.

To draw a crowd to the festival, he brought in big names: civil rights leader Julian Bond, photographer Gordon Parks, recording artist Arthur Prysock, and sports stars such as Wally Jones from the 76ers and Lenny Moore from the Baltimore Colts. Planning the festival took about half a year. They started planning in the fall of 1967, a time of growing racial tensions, and it was finally held in May of 1968, a month after the assassination of Martin Luther King. During the planning, people were concerned that the white community would not attend.

But that wasn't the case. The festival was well-attended—with about 85% of the attendees white—and 50,000 portions of food were handed out. The festival showed that by taking a stand, it allowed others to voice their support and opposition to bigotry.

knowing is understanding

This festival was the first Dad held with the theme *Knowing is Understanding*. There were many more to follow. In 1976, he actually wrote about these festivals.

Here's what he wrote:

The programs we're proudest of are what we call "Knowing is Understanding." The first we did was eight years ago, in 1968. It was a Black Heritage Program (the first in the country). Reading has a small black community—industrious, but with far fewer opportunities than whites. We tried to demonstrate the importance of black contribution to our culture in music, dance, art, photography, science, fashion, government, culinary arts, and sports. At the time, it was a controversial program and made for us a few enemies. But we believe it made for us many more friends.

Since that first program, we've done others. Festival de Puerto Rico was a similar program for our Spanish Speaking Community. When our local Blind Association was having difficulty in getting zoning approval for expansion of their workshop, we did a program on blindness. We called it "Broaden Your Vision. Blindness is Often in the Eyes of the Beholder."

In 1973, because of the confusion and misunderstanding about the women's movement by both men and women, we gathered together the leaders of the movement for an unforgettable program featuring Gloria Steinem, Letty Cottin Pogrebin, playwright Myrna Lamb, athlete Wilma Rudolph, and even original suffragette Florence Luscomb, who was 85 years old. It was great! We had bomb threats and no one would leave. The program was taped, and I still see portions of it on educational TV, almost every month. "Women Power" proved to be an exciting and educational program in understanding.

In July, when Americans were busy celebrating their 200th Anniversary and we were all pretty damn proud of ourselves, Boscov's did a bicentennial salute on the Native American and how they have fared after 200 years of U.S. rule. It was the best attended 4th of July program in the area.

A fringe benefit of our "Knowing is Understanding" programs is that I learn a lot. Boscov's is not afraid to take a stand on any issue that we believe will make our communities a better place in which to live.

I cherish that throughout my dad's 87 years he always "loved to learn a lot " and that he was never afraid to take a stand to make our community and our world a better place in which to live; in fact he saw this as one of his most important missions.

Joanne Barker

I began working with Boscov's in 1974. In 1977, the store manager I worked for approached me about setting up an interview with Albert for an assistant store manager position. There were only five Boscov's at the time, and being an assistant store manager was still a relatively new idea.

My boss informed me that I would not get the job, but the exposure to Albert and Ed would be good if a buying position opened up.

See, in 1977, men still tended to be chauvinistic. Apparently, women could be buyers but couldn't to go into store management.

Even when I called to set up an appointment, Albert's secretary assumed I was interviewing to be a buyer. When I told her, "No, I want to be an assistant store manager," there was complete silence until she regained her composure.

The day of my interview, I remember my knees shaking so badly that I was surprised I could stand. I entered Albert's office. My knees were still shaking. He asked me to sit. Then he went into a long story about Boscov's. When he was done, he sat back in his chair and said, "All right. Your turn to talk."

How do you respond to that?

When I was done telling him about my background, he proceeded to ask me every illegal question in the book.

He asked, "Are you married? Do you have children? Who will watch them?" He asked because he had three daughters, and the way he approached his life meant that he was at work a lot. I remember him telling me that it is the quality (and not the amount of time) you spend with your family that matters.

At the end of the interview, he told me if I didn't get the job, it wasn't because he was chauvinistic. He hoped his daughters would get ahead on their own merits in life and not be held back due to their gender. He then set up an interview for me with his business partner, Ed.

The very next day, I got the job.

After forty-three years with the company (and more than thirty as a store manager), that one encounter remains the reason for my utmost respect for Albert Boscov. Even when chauvinism was the norm, he believed someone's merits shouldn't be limited by their sex.

When he hired me, he told me that I didn't have to wait a year for a raise. He said as soon I started to be of use to the store manager, I would get my promotion.

A week before my anniversary as an assistant store manager, Albert visited the store. I reminded him of what he had said, and I added that as far as I was concerned, I was of use to the store manager the first week I started since I began right before Christmas. I'm pretty sure I made my point. I received an additional twenty dollars a week, and it was made retroactive for six months. In 1977, that was huge for me. It afforded me to have Santa deliver a few extra gifts for my children.

Connie Giesler

Boscov's was my first job after being a stay-at-home mom for 17 years. My daughter encouraged me to apply. She was a college student at the time, and Boscov's offered her a way to make the money she needed for all four years of her education. I started as a gift wrapper for the holiday season and, after the holidays, stayed on to work customer service. I loved working there—loved the coworkers and loved the customers. I moved up in the company, becoming a store trainer and then the HR manager at Woodbridge when it was opening.

I still remember opening weekend. I was in the store manager's office when Mr. B came in with a couple of executives. He was hungry. He asked someone to find him a snack, but he was even more concerned about finding a trailer full of missing meatloaf pans. They were giveaways to credit customers, and he simultaneously worked the phone, conversed with us, and snacked on an ice cream sandwich as he tried to find where 17,500 meatloaf pans went. He kept saying, "We have to find them. Our customers really love this product!"

My biggest thrill from that weekend was simply seeing him and hearing him say, "Thank you for being here." No, Mr. B. Thank you for giving this mom a chance to re-imagine a career after 17 years on the sidelines. I have moved on from retail. But every day I still carry the important lessons I learned from Mr. B.

Be honest with those you deal with. No matter what happens, they will appreciate your candor. Be kind to all you meet, and it will be returned to you. And always do the best you can to help others. Even if you cannot solve their problem, they will appreciate that you gave 100%.

Kim Thomas

There was never a dull moment cutting Mr. B's hair. He'd come in singing and dancing. I think I've been danced down the hallway fifteen or twenty times in a lifetime. I think the funniest story is from a few years ago. As he got older, his eyebrows got bigger and bigger. One time I said, "Would you like me to cut your eyebrows?"

He said, "Meh, I like them this way. They look like Albert Einstein's, and he's a brilliant man."

I said, "And so are you. We'll keep them."

The next time he came in, I asked, "Do you want me to trim your eyebrows?"

He said, "No, you know what? I'm getting a little bald on top. Let's comb my eyebrows back over my forehead, so nobody can see where I'm receding."

"Okay..."

The next time he came in, I asked him one last time, "Now, Mr. B, do you want me to trim your eyebrows?"

He said, "No. Eunice loves them this way."

"If your wife likes them like them...what can I say?"

With each passing week, his eyebrows got bushier and bushier.

One day, Eunice came into the salon with him and said, "Kim, would you mind cutting his eyebrows?! I don't understand why you haven't been cutting them."

I just looked at him and said, "Well, he seems to think you think they're sexy."

From that point on, I never asked. I just trimmed his eyebrows.

Diane Dautrich

It was a Saturday night. I was working in the very back of the handbag department, and I looked up, and there they were, Mr. and Mrs. Boscov, walking hand in hand down the store aisle. It was the cutest thing I have ever seen. I think they were going to the Greenery for dinner. They looked so adorable holding hands. You could just see how much they loved each other.

Joe McGrath

I used to be in charge of the TV and Appliance department. As larger scale appliance stores became more popular, our department stopped being profitable.

Mr. Boscov tried to find a way to keep the department—if only we could make a few more points of margin—and make a little profit.

So he and I spent three days in a car together, going to every single TV and appliance vendor. Every time we left a meeting, the first call Mr. Boscov would make was to his wife, Eunice.

He would say, "Hi, honey," and then he would go through everything that just happened in the meeting. I was only hearing one side of the call, but from his responses and tone, I was struck by how concerned and engaged Eunice was in the conversation.

He would say, "Yeah, I asked them that, and I asked them that, and they just weren't able to find any more money for us."

After the third day of driving to vendors and getting turned down by everyone, he called Eunice and told her, "I have a big decision to make, and it's going to weigh heavily on me."

There were around two hundred co-workers who would be affected if we decided to leave TV and appliances. Two hundred doesn't seem like a lot when there are about eight thousand employees. So when he told me, "We need to get out of appliances, but I don't want to lose a single co-worker," safe to say, I was amazed.

The compassionate and meticulous way Mr. Boscov left the appliance business has always stuck with me.

You know what he did?

He made room where there wasn't room. He said, "We'll expand the furniture department, and we'll give them options and accommodate them where we can."

Any other company would have let us go, but he found a place for everyone in my department. Thank goodness for that, because I'm still here and hopefully still making him proud.

Debbie Goodman

As a friend, Eunice is always peaceful, easy, comfortable, and fun to be with whether we're at an art show, shopping, or out to lunch. Albert's energy was always way up high, but Eunice was such a calming influence on him that kept his feet on the ground. What brought them together? I bet a lot of common ground and then that balance. They were ying and yang, Albert and Eunice.

Eunice Boscov

I had just graduated from Brooklyn College. Two girlfriends and I decided we wanted to meet guys—specifically, nice ones. We decided to go to the Green Mansion in the Adirondacks because it was a tennis camp; we didn't play tennis, but I guess we thought the guys who did would be nice.

One day, I was playing badminton with a guy I had met at dinner

when I noticed a fellow on the sidelines watching us play. He smiled a lot and seemed very pleasant. I thought he was waiting to use my racket. When we finished, I handed it to him.

He put it down and followed us to the lake, where he helped us into our canoe and then pushed us onto the water.

He started to jump up and down and wave to us from shore.

The guy I was with remarked, "What a nice guy!"

I thought so, too.

The fellow onshore was Al.

I didn't see Al for the rest of the day. Later he told me he had looked all over for me. The next morning, I was at breakfast when the hostess arrived with a note, requesting I go to the lobby.

Standing in the lobby was Al. I was very impressed with his politeness—that he didn't impose by coming to the table. He and I talked for a while. I told him I was an English major. He told me he wrote children's stories.

He asked for my phone number, and that's how Al and I started dating.

I lived in Flatbush, and he drove to see me. He joked it took him as long to park as it did to drive in from Reading. One of our first dates was to Atlantic City. I didn't know him that well, so I brought mad money, as we called it, in case I needed to get home on my own. We were walking on the pier when I got chilly. I opened my sweater, which is where I had tucked the money when I unpacked earlier. All of it fell in the water. Do you know what Al did? He climbed down the post of the pier and grabbed the money out of the water. People were standing around, cheering.

As we continued dating, I kept asking him "Where are these children's stories you write?" Eventually, he confessed that he didn't write for kids. I guess I forgave him for the white lie (because I still thought he was a pretty nice guy).

Our wedding was a year and a week after we first met. We married in September, 1959, and settled in Reading to be near his family and work.

Over time, our family and the store grew. By 1968, there were three stores in Reading (North, East, and West), and we had three little girls (Ruth, Ellen, and Meg). I took care of them while Al worked at the store, often for long hours.

When I was young, there was a mindset about what a man or a woman should do in life and for their family. Growing up, my father worked in a shipyard and then selling encyclopedias. His work took us from Brooklyn to Detroit, where I went to Cass Tech High School and studied art, and then back to Brooklyn when I was fifteen. There was an arts and music high school in the Bronx I wanted to attend, but at that point, I had no one guiding me, and I was scared to travel so far by myself, so I never enrolled. But I've always loved the arts.

When I was young, more often than not, people thought only men could get their art in museums or be recognized as artists. The men were also assumed to be the professors and the doctors, and we, or at least I, accepted that was the way it was supposed to be.

Early on in our marriage, one of Al's friends and his wife came to visit. I remember being surprised seeing that she was the one who had the camera and not her husband. Maybe I was extraordinarily

naïve, but for me, that was a light bulb moment.

In high school, I remember being required to draw outside and, being self-conscious, worrying people who were walking by might see my art or judge it. Photography really was the answer to my self-consciousness. I liked that when I looked into the lens, I was the only one who could see the image I framed.

Because of Al's friend's wife, I started taking pictures, first just of our family and the girls. I saw that I was good at it and that I enjoyed it, so I started taking classes at Kutztown University. Al was so proud of me and of my work. Another man might have been dismissive. He supported me. When we went on trips, he carried my cameras and my film. Our travels took us all over the world. He was always curious. Never impatient. He liked my work, and he was glad to see I was doing it.

My first photography show was at a gallery on Fifth Street in Reading. He arranged for a surprise party following the event. In the entranceway to our house, he placed a foam cardboard where people could sign their names.

I still have it, which is nice, because now I can look at it and remember back...

The card read, "A picture is worth a thousand words."

photo courtesy of Cappy Hotchkiss Photography

We all went with Granddaddy to the doctors to figure out what was wrong—his wife, daughters, and grandchildren. Granddaddy joked that it was like that scene in the Marx Brothers movie. Everyone's jammed into a room that's too small until the door bursts open and they flood out into the hallway.

We ended up back at the house, knowing now that Granddaddy had a month to live. He asked us to walk with him through the art he and Eunie had collected over almost sixty years. We began in the family room. A tile portrait of Rembrandt was hanging over the fireplace.

"Hello, Rembrandt," Granddaddy said. Then he told us the story behind the portrait. He and Eunie had seen it in a little antique shop in Reading a year or two after they married. Eunie had told him how much she liked it, but he told her they couldn't afford it. They had just signed on their first house. A few days later, Rembrandt was waiting when she opened the door. Granddaddy was laughing, telling us about it.

After Rembrandt, he walked slowly from room to room. He studied each painting with a special focus, as if looking through them, into an adventure with Eunie that he knew he wouldn't be able to share with us for very much longer. .

Then he said, "Now this is from our honeymoon, in Haiti." And Eunie said, "No, no, Al, that's from Barbados." For every piece there was a story (or two) of where he and Eunie were when they found it, in the world, but also in their lives.

A month later, the last words I heard him speak told the same story, of what mattered most to him, just straight to the point. *I love Eunie Boscov,* he said. *I love Eunie Boscov so much.*

Michael Cuello

One thing that I will always remember is when my second daughter was born. I was just the new guy here. I was a little hesitant to ask for extra time, so the very next day I came to work. I got a call from Mr. B asking why I came in.

He said, "Take care of your baby; take care of your wife." He even sent me an email telling me to take as much time as I needed. I keep that email on my wall.

Five years later, after I had my third daughter, he asked, "How are the babies doing?"

I said, "Good, good."

He asked, "Do you tell them that you love them every day?"

And I was like, "Yeah, you know."

And he was like, "I mean it. Tell all three of them that you love them every day because I have three daughters, too."

I said I would follow his advice, which I haven't done as well as I could.

After he passed, I thought, "Darn it, I'm going to do what Mr. B told me and tell my daughters that I love them every day."

That's the way to appreciate what he did...by emulating him.

My dad and I were driving to the Reading airport. I was sitting next to my father in the front seat of his station wagon, holding his hand as I held back my tears. I was ready to go back to the excitement of college, but it was always emotional to leave my parents' loving home.

My dad usually makes it easy to leave tears behind, but today instead of singing nonsense songs or making up ridiculous tall tales as he drove, he engaged me in a serious conversation.

You could always tell when my dad was going to discuss a serious topic because when he did, the corners of his lips would turn down, as if his cheeks were weighed down by a thought or sadness. So there we were, the two of us, and the surrounding countryside.

It seemed as if there was no one else in the world.

He began, "Ruthie, you seem to really love anthropology and get genuinely excited by intellectual ideas. That's wonderful."

He continued to speak of his career in retailing and how he got excited by "making things happen" and that he loved what he was doing. He said, of course, he would welcome me into Boscov's, but that I should choose a career that I really love.

He said, "Ruthie, you need to find a career that makes you happy, so you go to work each day thrilled to do what you do. I have found that, and I want you to find that, too." There they were—the words that made all the difference in my life.

do what you love

and you'll love what you do

He wasn't going to pressure me to find a career to please him or Mom. He wouldn't feel hurt if I didn't enter the family business. I was to find a job that would make me happy. So my search began, a search free from pressures and parental expectations. I dabbled in careers in anthropology, social work, human resources, and concert production, until I finally found my love as a teacher and educator.

Along the way, my father lived up to his words; he was truly supportive of each endeavor, and his love and support made the difference to help me to find a career and a life that I love.

Meg Boscov

When I was a girl, I was painfully shy. My mother recalls her sadness and surprise when the day camp counselor told her at the end of the summer that I had not said a single word to anyone the entire eight weeks. Clearly I had not inherited my father's extroverted nature, but I do credit my father for teaching me by example how to come out of my shell.

My dad's extroversion came from a sincere interest in and empathy for each and every person he met. Up until the last days of his life, he expressed more concern for the people around him—from his family to the nurses and doctors who cared for him—than he did for himself.

My dad taught me that each person has a story, and if we are open and kind, we will be fortunate enough to hear a multitude of rich, beautiful stories in our life. Thank you, Dad. My life is indeed richer by striving to live by your example. I no longer want to hide away, when I know that living fully is stepping outside of yourself to look into the eyes of someone you love, or even someone you just met. Every encounter is an opportunity to learn, to grow, to empathize, to laugh, and to experience and share this life together. I picture my dad on one of our treasured family trips to the Caribbean. He's wearing his *Don't Worry Be Happy* shirt. We are holding hands as he sings, hugs, and jumps up and down with everyone we meet. Oh and how wonderful are the stories we hear!

Amelia Xanthe Boscov

When I was about to start my first year in middle school, I was scared I would get lost in all of the new, big, scary buildings. I had nightmares about it. I even cried to my mom, wishing I could just stay in elementary school. I was not ready for the change.

A week before the school year started, I went to my grandparents' house. It was a beautiful, warm summer's day, so I wanted to go play in my grandparents' huge backyard. Before I could go outside, my grandfather (or as I called him, my Granddaddy Al) handed me a boatswain's whistle that he used when he was in the Navy. He told me about how vast their backyard was, and how tall the plants grew, and how it might be easy to get lost out there. But he also told me that I shouldn't worry because if I did get lost, I could just blow this whistle, and he would be able to find me. My granddaddy is a master adventurer, so I knew I could trust him.

I went on to wear the whistle he gave me every day of the school year. I would lead my friends around the middle school, bragging how we couldn't get lost because my granddaddy would be able to find us. My friends began to add to the story, agreeing that he would probably come riding in on a big white horse—or maybe even on a flying car—to our rescue if we ever needed it. To this day, I still wear his whistle whenever I need some granddaddy courage.

Jonah Boscov-Brown

I remember getting into the pool and never wanting to get out because Granddaddy would always keep me busy and entertained. He would take my hands and spin me around, or I would get in an inflatable raft, and he would push me along in the water. While we would be in the pool he would also tell me amazing stories, some true, some very entertaining, silly lies; it was always fun trying to figure out which stories were real.

Swimming with Granddaddy was not all about silliness; there was also work. Each time I got in the pool, I got a swimming lesson from Granddaddy. I would start on one side of the pool, and he would be next to me. He would always go first, so he could show me how to do the strokes, and then it would be my turn. I had to swim a full length of the pool while Granddaddy followed me and observed my technique. When I would get a stroke right, Granddaddy would be so happy it would make me want to practice more. He put so much time and effort into making sure I was a good swimmer that I couldn't let him down. Even to this day, I think of the advice I was taught by my granddaddy. I still picture him teaching me freestyle and saying, "Just pretend you're scooping up the water."

Christine Miller

I have a memory of Mr. Boscov that I will forever hold dear to my heart. One day while walking on the selling floor at the East store, I encountered Mr. Boscov scolding a young coworker whose mother had come to visit. She had been rude to her mom, and Mr. B gave her a short lecture on respect. I continued on with a smile and a permanent reminder to remember to be kind to others no matter what mood I might be in. He really was family to us.

Jacob Stein

In September of 2014, I had my first phone conversation with Albert and Jim Boscov. I was working in Cleveland, Ohio. There was an opportunity for me to join Boscov's as they were looking for a real estate person. While I questioned the move as everyone talked about the "dying future" of department stores, I was excited about the idea as my then boss assured me that working at Boscov's was second to none. So, I connected with Jim and Albert, and the memory of a lifetime began.

I enjoyed fifteen of the most memorable minutes of my life, talking—well, mostly listening—to the most energetic and passionate man I had ever encountered. I assumed Jim was going to do most of the talking because I knew Albert was eighty-five.

To my surprise, Albert took hold of the phone and kept on talking without ever seeming to take a breath. Though I couldn't

treat everyone like family

see him, I could hear the passion and energy he had for retail. He talked about trends, competition, sales for each store, sales of each competitor, why Boscov's was thriving, why others were struggling, and about the whacky sales and events unique to Boscov's.

While I'm typically skeptical by nature, I had just been sold on the idea of uprooting my life and moving to Reading within fifteen minutes by a man I had never met. I was going to work for a company I barely knew in a city I had never been to.

Following our call, I was asked to come to Reading for a visit. But I wasn't allowed to come unless my wife came as well. I didn't know what to make of this–bringing your wife to an interview? What kind of interview was this?

While I pondered these questions then, I would later realize that this is the single greatest attribute Al leaves behind and one that Jim carries forward: treat everyone like family.

They wanted me to bring my wife so that they could welcome her and show her the wonderful things Reading has to offer, and to assure her that she would like it here. My wife and I quickly realized that Al's open-arm friendliness was the norm for Boscov's. We quickly joined an extremely long list of individuals that fell for him and the company from the moment we met him.

Diana Thomas

I lost both of my grandfathers before I was born. When I started working for Boscov's, I got the grandfather I never had. Albert was an amazingly personable man with a spirit that could light up any room.

Three years ago, I was pregnant. Some days, I felt like he was more excited to meet my daughter than I was, if that's even possible! A week before I was due, he saw me waddling down the hallway and stopped me. He said in a very serious voice, "Diana, how did this happen?" He then said, with a chuckle, "You guys have been busy, haven't you?" I didn't know whether to cry or to die of laughter! (Pregnancy hormones were kicking in).

A day or so later, we had a big meeting. I'm a table linen buyer, and I was presenting on table linens that we had bought that year. During the meeting, Albert turned to me and said, "Diana, you better have a good year. You want your daughter to be proud of you, don't you?" That's just the kind of guy Albert was. Always making us laugh. Always trying to get the best result from us while simply loving us!

One last memory. When my daughter was born, I would bring her in to see him. He was the absolute best with kids. I once brought her in, and he just grabbed her right out of my arms and started singing and dancing with her. He then walked her over to his office and gave her a big bag of candy. Mind you she was barely a one-year old and couldn't even eat it! He just had the biggest heart. He always told me how beautiful she was and how I did such a great job creating such a beautiful human being.

Albert was not only a grandfather figure to me, but he was a great-grandfather figure to my daughter. She always said, "Al, Al," whenever she was at the store because she always wanted to see him.

George Chow

My father owned the Peking Restaurant near the Fairgrounds Square Mall. It was probably in the late '70s. I was maybe seven years old. I remember looking up at a big man with a powerful voice that would come in to talk to my father. The man said, "Mr. Chow, I only have daughters and no sons to take over my business. You have four boys. Why don't you give me one of your sons, and I'll give you the North store?"

My dad would play along, "Sure, take my youngest."

Well that was me.

So every time Mr. B came in for take-out, he would ask my dad, "Mr. Chow, are you ready to make the exchange?"

My dad would say yes, and I would assume the position: me wrapped around my dad's leg, crying thinking this big man was going to take me away.

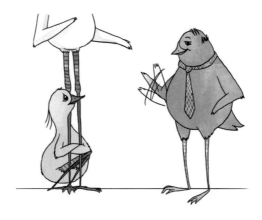

If you told me I was going to work for the man who *terrorized* me as a child, I would have said you were nuts. Yet here I am. I am honored and humbled that I have had the opportunity to work for my dad's longtime friend, and I take comfort knowing that they've been reunited.

They're probably sharing a good laugh right now as I'm telling you this story.

Santo D. Marabella

My dad still tells the story of how one Christmas Eve, when a wheel on my X-15 tricycle was missing, he came in to Boscov's North, and Mr. B scoured the store to find a replacement. All were sold out. Mr. B told him that my dad could take any toy for me.

Dad also remembers a serviceman doing some last-minute shopping. Mr. B told that serviceman that he could come back after Christmas and pay for everything when his paycheck came in. Fifty years later, dad still remembers Mr. B's kindness.

Over the years, as I grew up and became more involved in the community and the arts, whether it was a program for shut-ins, an original TV pilot, a play, the film commission, a film festival, or most recently, putting on the work of Lynn Nottage, Mr. B always found a way to support this wide-eyed do-gooder.

Thank you, Mr. B, from myself and from my father, Sam Marabella.

I had the honor of working for Mr. Boscov in the Vineland store for over sixteen years. At one time or another, all four of my children worked at the same store, and we share fond memories. One moment comes sharply to mind. When my oldest son was a junior in college, he wrote to Mr. B to tell him of the venture that he and a group of classmates would be embarking upon over spring break. They were going to Appalachia to rebuild a soup kitchen and were looking for donations to cover the cost of gas and lodging for the trip. Less than a week later, a letter appeared in my son's college mailbox with a personal check from Mr. B for $500.00—more than enough to cover the gas. This was just the way Mr. B was. Generous to a fault.

Gene London

I hosted a children's TV program in Philadelphia called, "Cartoon Corner's General Store," which was also known as, "The Gene London Show." Creatively, it was heaven. I played all of the parts.

One minute, I was an evil witch, cursing, "I'll fix you!" The next minute, I was a fair princess weeping or a lumbering giant. I drew pictures for the kids as I told stories. The show was an overnight sensation. Every kid in the Philadelphia area watched it.

Not long after my show went on the air, I got a phone call from a man who told me, "My kids love your show, and I love it, too. Can we come for a visit?"

I got tickets for the man and his children and arranged for his three daughters to stand beside me at the drawing board while I told a story. The kids had such a good time that they came back many times.

One day, the man, whom I knew simply as Al, called me and said, "Gene, I'd like to bring 'Cartoon Corners' to my store in Reading."

I said, "You have a store in Reading? Is it near Renninger's?" (Renninger's was one of my favorite places to go antiquing). As soon as I learned Al was near Renninger's, I agreed to perform at his store.

The day of the show, Al's longtime secretary Vivian welcomed me warmly and brought me down to the auditorium. Al was waiting outside the room. He said, "Gene, listen."

We put our ears to the door. Inside we could hear the room abuzz with kids laughing and talking.

He said, "It's packed. Are you ready?"

I said, "Introduce me," and then I did my show, which was fabulous.

Al asked me to come back time and again. I always did because it was such fun and because I enjoyed seeing Al and shopping at Renninger's.

When my television show ended, I did costuming in Manhattan for many years and lost touch with Al. I opened a store on 5th Avenue, where I sold antiques and dresses. Unfortunately, after 9/11, the fashion world suffered, and I could no longer afford the retail space. I had so many costumes and dresses of historical and personal significance. I didn't know what to do.

I happened to run into Al. I told him about my predicament. He said, "Come to Reading. There are a lot of opportunities here, and I'll be your fairy godmother."

Those were his words: my fairy godmother.

I took his advice and moved to Reading. He found warehouse and studio space for me in one of his best buildings and never charged rent. We worked on so many exciting projects together.

After he passed, I asked Vivian, "Why did Al love me so?"

She said, "Gene, don't you know how much you meant to Albert? He never forgot those early years when you would visit the stores and entertain the kids."

I think we were kindred spirits, Al and me. He was a kid, and so am I. That's the best gift God can give you—to be a kid. I can see Al singing in my mind! Or doing a happy dance. He never lost his well of immaturity. We think of immaturity as a horrible word, but I think immaturity is like heartstrings that pop out of you when you're at your happiest. Like so many others I am blessed for having known Al and forever grateful for his generosity and friendship.

Patrick Cassidy

I was working in Las Vegas, as the artistic director of ShowStoppers, when my mother called me. She said, "Honey, I've been asked to do another Boscov's store opening, and I have to tell you—it's two shows a day, eight days—I just don't have the energy to perform sixteen shows all on my own." Before she hung up, she added, "I'll give you ten thousand out of my salary to do the show with me."

I told her I'd do it for free, but she insisted and thanked me for helping.

So I came home.

This was in the fall of 2015 for the Meriden store opening. We didn't have a huge amount of time for rehearsal. I think we had four days to take her act, restructure it, and combine it with mine. We infused all of the work she had done in movies (*Oklahoma*, *The Music Man*, *Carousel*), with all of the work I had done in theater, so it became a mother-son presentation about the careers of Shirley

Jones and Patrick Cassidy. In hindsight, what we created together was better than me doing my show alone, or her doing her show alone, because it allowed the audience an insight into our mother-son relationship.

From what I understand, Mr. Boscov did not usually attend the shows at his store openings. For our first performance, there he was in the front row, with two of his daughters and a grandson. That threw me. He was there with his family.

The show began, and my mother and I sang, and we told stories from our careers. The show shined, not because it was about me or about my mother, but because it was a look at the two of us, as mother and son. We got to the moment toward the end of the show where I sang, "Mama, a rainbow," which is about the mother in your life, who has given you everything, including your being here on this planet. As I was singing, I looked over, and there were tears streaming down Mr. Boscov's face. I was so touched that he was moved by our performance.

After the show, he couldn't have been more gracious or complimentary. He was so thrilled with what we had given him. His attention during the show and his words of appreciation already meant so much, but after our last show on the last day, he went above and beyond, and I'll never forget it.

I was in the car with my mother when she received a call from Mr. Boscov.

She listened. Then said, "Uh-huh, Patrick's right here..."

She handed me the phone. Mr. Boscov thanked me again for what we had done and for what we had given him.

He said, "I've heard your mother has compensated you. But I'd like to compensate you more."

In my whole life, no producer has ever told me, "I'm going to give you more money," especially after everything is all said and done. He didn't owe me a dime.

He ended up sending me another ten thousand dollars. I was absolutely floored. I would have been happy with anything because it wasn't about the money.

The money helped me pay a lot of bills, which I appreciated a lot, but really I was just blown away by his generosity. I've now told this story many times to many people. I've never experienced anything like it before in my life.

Sometimes, what you do when nothing is required of you speaks so much about who you are. I think he did it out of the kindness and generosity of his heart because he didn't want my salary weighing on my mother and was moved by our mother-son performance. He knew it was more meaningful than if either of us had performed alone.

I just can't tell you how much it meant to me. It was a one-of-a-kind gesture from a one-of-a-kind guy.

Irene Kelly

Eunice tells a story. She and Al had only been dating for a few months.

They were traveling through the mountains to go skiing in Vermont when they saw an accident on the side of the road. Al pulled over. He took a blanket from his trunk and gave it to the injured motorist. In retelling this story, Eunice said, "Al always had a blanket for anyone in need." I thought that was beautiful.

After Al passed, someone posted the story about Al and the blanket story on Facebook. I saw it and thought, "We need to do a blanket drive." I felt that need because I had worked with him for years, in the store and in opening the Kirby.

The Kirby is another wonderful story. In Wilkes-Barre, the Paramount Theater was a grand movie house that fell into disrepair in the 1970s. The building was gutted, on the verge of demolition, when Albert intervened. To thank the community for making Wilkes-Barre Boscov's one of the company's top dollar stores, Albert

led a charge to renovate the theater, renaming it the F.M. Kirby Center for the Performing Arts. To this day, there is a plaque in the Kirby thanking Albert for accomplishing the impossible in saving the theater.

He did so much for other people, and that's why I wanted to do the blanket drive, to show his compassion and good will lives on.

On September 22nd, 2017 (which was the beginning of fall and what would have been Albert's 88th birthday), we held our first "A blanket from Al" charity drive for the homeless in the four stores that I am the Public Relations manager: Wilkes-Barre, Hazelton,

Scranton and Pottsville. We hope to do a blanket drive for many years, in memory of Al and his selflessness in helping others.

always have a blanket for someone in need

Ed McKeaney

I was thirty years old and having health issues. I got a call at the office that the neurologist I had seen thought I might have MS. The doctor told me that they wanted to put me in the hospital for extensive tests.

I asked, "When?"

The doctor said, "Tomorrow."

I went to see Albert to tell him. He was at a meeting, so I spoke with Gerry Floto, who was then his secretary.

She said, "What's the matter, honey?"

I told her what was wrong, and that I wouldn't be able to work ads with him today or tomorrow because I'd be in the hospital all morning.

I added, "So I just wanted to let him know that I can't make our meeting...because I have to go home to tell my wife."

I went home around one o' clock. At the time, my wife and I had two little babies. She and I were commiserating about the future when, around four o' clock, the doorbell rang.

It was Albert. He found out where I lived and came to see how I was doing. He stayed for two hours just to entertain us. We laughed like crazy the whole time.

When he left, he gave me a hug and said, "Everything will be all right. You know, I love you. " I was in the hospital three or four days. Every day I was in the hospital, either Albert, Eunice, Ed, or Alma Lakin called to make sure I was okay. I'm now well and still working at the store thirty-plus years later.

Paul O. Reber

I met Mister Boscov once when his mother was in the Reading Rehabilitation hospital up the hill on Route 10. I was an orderly, and he was taking mom for a stroll in her wheelchair. I noticed that the wheelchair had a loose or maladjusted foot pedal and commenced to sit on the floor to fix it. He did not hesitate to sit on the floor to lend assistance. Just a moment in time, so long ago, but also a summary of his life as the community saw him—always ready and willing to help us.

Dayle Sensenig Bitting

Back around 1979-1980, my parents went on a trip through Boscov's travel to the Dominican Republic. Neither of my parents, both in their mid-sixties, had ever flown before. Within hours of arriving in the Dominican Republic, my father suffered a stroke, which the doctors felt was the result of flying. My parents were in a strange country in a strange hospital with strange doctors all around them and had no idea what was going to happen next. Who came to their rescue? Al Boscov. He covered all of their additional expenses and made sure that they were able to get back home when my father was healthy enough to travel. Unbelievable. Both of my parents are now gone, but they never failed to tell the story of how Al helped them feel comforted when they truly needed it.

Pauline Henry

Seventeen years ago, my brother fell at work and was rushed to the ER. The doctors informed my parents that my brother's colon cancer, which we thought had been caught early on, had progressed so much that it was just a matter of time. The doctors couldn't even promise a single day. My parents tried to reach me at work, but I was helping open the Butler store, and they had no way to contact me. Being unaware of what was happening at home, I went with the group straight from the store out to dinner, arriving back at the hotel slightly after eleven at night. There were several messages left for me to call home immediately. I began calling every one of my family members only to get no answer. I was sick to my stomach and worried terribly.

In the morning, I tried again but still no answer.

When I arrived at the store, Angela Updike from HR told me that my parents had been calling and that I needed to call the number that they had left immediately because there had been a family emergency.

I sat down and called only to hear the dreadful words that my oldest brother, my hero, was going to die and that I needed to get home ASAP in order to see him alive. I just sat there and cried.

I didn't know how I was going to get home in time because I hadn't even driven. I came with everyone in the group van.

As I was walking out of the office, Angela and Mr. Boscov walked in. He put his arm around me and, with the kindest words I ever heard, asked me what was going on. I told him.

He shared with me how he had lost a sister to cancer, as well. He then asked who drove and if that person could drive me back to the hotel to get my personal belongings. I was so confused that I didn't know what was happening. Even after he told me, I was in shock.

He asked what was the nearest airport that I needed to fly into! He then asked how I felt about flying with the buyers and executives. Before I could answer, he said, "Never mind, I'll have my pilot fly in with the smaller plane to take you home."

Because of this wonderful, amazing man, I was able to spend my brother's last hours with him. As I sit here writing this, I have tears rolling down my face. I know I could never repay him for what he did. No money in this world can replace the time he gave me to spend with my brother. My time and my loyalty to his company were all I could ever give back. I have been employed with Boscov's for almost twenty years and counting, as a department manager of the home furnishings department at the Vineland store. Mr. B will forever be in my heart.

Tom McMahon

I was the mayor of Reading from 2004 to 2012. When I was first elected, Albert came into my office, and we talked about our ideas for the revitalization of downtown. In 2000, he started the non-profit, Our City Reading, which also sought to revitalize downtown; so Albert had his ideas, and I had mine. The more I talked about my plans without acknowledging his hopes and dreams for the city, the more nervous he became to the point that he actually got up and put on his coat.

He said, "If you don't need my help, that's fine. I'll be on my way."

I got up, and I put an arm around him. We knew each other well, but not as well as we would after eight years of working together in the community.

I said, "I love you, Albert. Now come back, so we can work this out."

When I got elected, I thought *I* could change the world, but in that moment, I realized he had more ideas than anyone else, and the drive and contacts to get things done. We did it differently than I initially planned, but we accomplished more because I worked with him.

One of the most successful programs that his nonprofit promoted was a home ownership initiative for first-time home buyers. Too often slumlords charge high rents, resulting in families abandoning their residences. Our City Reading sought to make home ownership affordable and a point of pride and stability for the city. From 2000 to 2017, Our City Reading remodeled 575 abandoned homes for first-time home buyers. The houses Albert got came to us through HUD for a dollar or for half of their evaluation. They generally were a mess but Albert could see past the trash to their potential.

By the time Garreth Donly, Our City Reading's Director of Construction, fixed them up, the houses looked fantastic. They had new floors and walls, and all new appliances. Everything was remodeled.

I remember going on tours before the houses were renovated. I was terrified. Albert, in his late seventies, climbed rickety steps and maneuvered crawl spaces that had exposed asbestos and walls with lead paint. By three in the afternoon, we had seen several houses. My back was hurting, so I sat down. But Albert was still going.

I said, "Albert, why don't you take a break?"

He said, "Tom, how old are you?"

"I'm ten years younger than you are."

That's all he needed to say. I got up, and I kept working. He was the hardest-working, happiest guy I ever knew.

Carrie Neiswender

For the first few years, every time a new homeowner moved into a house that we fixed up, Albert, Garreth Donly, and I went door-to-door. I remember Albert's usual greeting. The door would open, and he would say, "Hi, I'm Al Boscov! We're having a party this weekend. There will be food, drinks, and you'll get to meet your new neighbors."

Everybody in the neighborhood would show up at these "Meet the Neighbor" parties. The mayor would be there, as would Vivian, who was Albert's executive assistant even after he retired from retail in 2005.

Once everyone had food and drink, we would introduce everyone and say everybody should know each other. We also presented the owner with new pots and pans donated by Boscov's. Then Albert would tell a story about his childhood and how everyone in the neighborhood used to know everyone including the neighborhood dog.

He would say, "That was Johnny Smith's little dog, and if you did something wrong, there was always somebody's grandmother who would get you in trouble."

Then he would talk about drug dealing in the neighborhood and how it's your neighborhood and if you see activity in the streets, you need to say something to your neighborhood grandma.

One time, Vivian and I were waiting outside of a church. Wherever we fixed up homes, we also partnered with the neighborhood churches. Albert believed if we got the churches to come together, we would inspire the community to work together as well. So we were waiting outside the church when Albert arrived in his wood-paneled station wagon. I don't know how he did it, but he exited the car, bent over, and split the seat of his pants—not a little tear but a massive one that left his boxer shorts hanging out.

He said, "Uh. Oh. This isn't good."

Vivian and I escorted him into the church basement.

We found a stapler and Frankensteined his pants. It was quick fix, not a good one. He put on his pants and said, "Well, I'm just going to have to keep my jacket on, so nobody sees."

Off he went to the front of the church. Vivian and I sat in the front pew and watched on as he did his usual spiel. As he talked, he began to sweat—a lot. It was ninety-five degrees out and there was no air conditioning. He stumbled through his speech about his childhood and Johnny Smith's little dog. He began to lose his train of thought. I thought, "This is not good."

He was beginning to talk about the neighborhood grandma when the heat simply became too much. He took off his coat and, to a church full of people, he said, "I'm sorry to tell everyone, but I split the @$% of my pants."

Vivian and I were like, "Oh my!"

"I'll just have to show you."

He turned around and showed his backside full of staples.

The whole church erupted in laughter.

I had just started working with him. I thought, "Wow, this is going to be a roller-coaster."

What resulted from that meeting was that the church elected somebody from the neighborhood to be the "neighborhood grandma," the spokesperson for the neighborhood.

A year or two later, it was nice to return to the neighborhood and see that the houses had put out little window planters that we had handed out at the "Meet the Neighbor" parties. Suddenly, there were flowers in the neighborhood. We found that if one house looked nice, it caught on to the next house, and that was his idea from the start; if we take pride in our communities and give somebody a home, that pride will spread throughout the neighborhood.

Adam Mukerji

For seventeen years, Albert sought to redevelop downtown. Everything—from the Doubletree Hotel to Entertainment Square, with its Imax Theater, the GoggleWorks Center for the Arts, the Second and Washington Garage and the neighboring GoggleWorks Apartments—were projects I worked on with him. Originally, the City of Reading had plans to turn the site that became the GoggleWorks Center for the Arts into a parking lot.

Albert and I said, "Nuh-huh. No way."

We took a page out of Governor Rendell's book. When he was mayor of Philadelphia, he created the Avenue of the Arts, and the redevelopment of the city bloomed around the arts district. We planned to do the same: foster the arts, with the hope that people would return to the city for entertainment.

In 2003, Albert and I went to city council to show them our plans for the GoggleWorks Art Center. The meeting was supposed to begin at 9 p.m. By the time the meeting was over, it was well past midnight. I insisted I take Albert home because whenever he drove, the lamppost would suddenly jump into the middle of the road.

By the time we got to his house in Glen Oley, it was one in the morning. Albert refused to let me leave at that hour.

His wife Eunice said, "Adam, it's late."

She got me a glass of water, a magazine and fresh towels. I called my wife to let her know where I was and that Albert and Eunice were taking good care of me.

I'm an early riser so the next morning, I got up at six only to discover Albert was already finished with his morning swim and was waiting for me with a milk jug in hand, wanting to know what cereal I liked. They welcomed me with such warmth and hospitality.

There are two things I learned from Albert over the years. One is humility. The other is to be kind to people, irrespective of their stature in life.

Of all the other projects Albert and I worked on over the years, Our City Reading's home ownership program was the most memorable. When people lose their homes to bank foreclosure or tax delinquency, they abandon them, causing the buildings to become dilapidated. These abandoned homes are a blight on the community, and neighboring houses lose their value. We would gut these foreclosed homes and put in new kitchens, new bathrooms, new everything. For five hundred dollars a month, instead of renting from a slumlord, a first-time homeowner could afford to take up permanent residence in the city. We did a lot of good, but there were days when even Albert's optimism faltered. I remember him saying, "There's so much hate. A Hispanic family moves in, and a white family moves out. When a black family moves in, the Hispanic family goes."

One day, he told me a story about how he and his dad, after work, carried bags of money two blocks for the night drop.

I said, "Two blocks? On North Ninth Street?"

He said, "We had nothing to fear because we knew everyone. The neighbors waved to us as my dad and I walked two blocks to the bank."

We live in a different time, but one thing is certain—if the world had more Albert Boscovs, it would be a kinder place to live in.

close your eyes and dream a little

In working with Albert, I learned the true meaning of doing by "sheer will." He projected a virtual reality around his projects, where everything was already built and operating.

As an early investor in the Doubletree Hotel, I remember him showing me hotel blueprints, where there was a multistory garage paid for by the state and costed by the square foot, with an operating budget and even a General Manager in place.

At every meeting, he would go over how the financial support from the state and, more specifically, how Ed Rendell's support made the decision a "no-brainer." He wanted us to believe that we couldn't lose.

For the Goggleworks Arts Center project, he flew a few of us to Greenville, South Carolina to show off what an inspired Redevelopment Board could do to bring a city back to life. On a rickety twin engine plane, he presented architectural drawings of entire city blocks rendered as if it were a *fait accompli* while the rest of us hung on for dear life.

When we landed, I was ready to give anything out of thanks for still being alive.

He really had me well sized-up from the moment he met me. I remember the first time he called me. The entire office was abuzz.

"Mr. Boscov's on the phone." The excitement was palpable.

That call was the first of what became many asks for my financial support and, progressively, for my time, as well. He knew my giving history and never had a qualm asking for the moon, always pushing beyond my comfort zone. I always felt it was a privilege and an honor to be asked by Albie to support his various pet projects. That big-hearted little man cast a spell on me, like he did on everyone.

For the Doubletree Hotel, I remember visiting multiple interior designers with him until he found his match in Baltimore. We found a talented woman, who gave us our beautifully designed treasure in downtown Reading.

I also remember feeling strongly about creating an active lobby for the hotel. Both she and I argued a great deal about it with him since it would require architectural changes.

It is true, when you gave input, you never knew if he considered it or not until ultimately the project was built. Albie was independent, headstrong, and opinionated. But I learned he took a lot in, and he synthesized it.

Following the financial meltdown, Boscov's bankruptcy, his return to Boscov's, the imminent change in state leadership, and the building of a new Sweet Street plant in Greenville, I felt I had to drop out of the hotel project—too much stress. I knew I was disappointing him, and it hurt.

At that point, I truly never thought the hotel would come to pass. But I learned you never could underestimate Albert Boscov. On the day of the grand opening of the Doubletree Hotel, as I walked in for my personal tour with Albie, I felt a sense of awe, respect, and quiet pride in my small contribution to its creation.

He was a legend like no other, who I will always love, respect, and emulate.

Before I met Mr. Boscov, I heard about this potential hotel, and I thought, "No way they get it up and running. In a city like Reading? Some management company will come in, and they'll do what they always do: bail it out, and the third owner will buy it for four cents on the dollar."

I don't think anybody thought the downtown Doubletree would happen, and I certainly didn't think I'd be running it. But Albert had a way of convincing people to believe in his vision. He got the funding, and we started construction in late 2013. Every Tuesday, the architect, the foreman, the builders, myself, and Albert met to discuss construction.

The day the bathroom fixtures arrived, Albert saw them, and he asked, "How big is the bathroom?"

Shower stalls are typically thirty inches. That's industry standard. Albert got in his mind that thirty inches didn't seem right. At this point in time, the frame of the hotel was already up, and we were putting in steel. He had his businesses, his nonprofit, and the newest Boscov's opening in Utica to concern himself with, but with all the things going on in his life, he was laser-focused on the size of the bathroom shower stall.

He kept saying, "Thirty inches? I don't know."

To appease him, we built a bathroom in the construction trailer out of Styrofoam to dimension. I still get chills thinking about it. He entered that trailer. He walked into the Styrofoam stall, and he stood there where the shower head would be, and he looked

around, and he had plenty of space.

Yet he said, "It's not big enough."

Everyone tried to convince him that it was standard size and fine.

He insisted, "Look. If a big man is standing here, or a large woman is taking a shower, and it's not comfortable for them, will they come back?"

Mr. Boscov was a small man. Yet in his mind, he was visualizing a person who was three or four times his size. The construction company reminded him that the plumbing and drains were already in place.

Again, he said. "But will they come back?"

He added, "If they don't return, we built this big hotel—why? It will become a hospital or an old folk's home, and I don't want that. I want people to want to return to the hotel and to be proud that it's in Reading."

He was right. We ended up putting in a 125 thousand dollar change order, so we could move the drains and build out another two inches. If you read reviews online, you'll notice people talk about how the bathroom is wonderful. They know there's something different about it. But they don't realize it's the difference between a thirty-inch and a thirty-two-inch bathtub. That difference may seem insignificant if you're not customer-centric. Not many people are customer or even employee-centric anymore, and he was both. He didn't have to report to a board of directors. He reported to himself, and nobody was guiding him, except his heart, his pulse, his soul, and his experience.

His bottom line was never, "What's the margin? How much will we make?"

It was always, "Will they come back?"

Governor Ed Rendell

In my almost forty years in politics, I have met a lot of persuasive people, but I have never met a better salesman than Al Boscov. I don't mean "salesman" necessarily in a business sense. There's the saying, "He could sell ice to Eskimos..."

Al could, except he never sold anything that he didn't believe in. That's what made him such a great salesman. His passion imbued you with his belief that his projects would succeed.

The first time I met Al was in 2001 when I was running for governor.

Somebody told me, "You have to meet Al Boscov."

I called him up.

The city of Reading is an hour northwest of Philadelphia, so Al already knew of me from my time as mayor.

He said, "I'd love to help you, but first come to Reading. I have something to show you."

We didn't meet at his office. He gave me an address to a vacant lot. The first thing I noticed about Al was his height. Here was this small man standing in a lot that was the size of a square city block.

The next thing I noticed about Al Boscov was his enthusiasm. That night, I went home and told my wife, "Honey, today I met an incredible elf."

More than his height, I was referring to his energy and outlook. To him, that lot wasn't dirt and debris. It had history. He loved stories, and he told them to make his point. The property we were standing on once belonged to a manufacturing business that either moved out of town or went out of business. No developer would build on the abandoned lot because it was polluted. Reading had many sites like this one, and this wasn't just a problem in Reading. There were sites like it across the state, with great locations, near railroads and highways, but no developer would touch them because of the cost of environmental remediation. Al told me, "If elected, your job will be to get sites like this one developed. To create jobs."

This is what resulted from that meeting with Al.

In my first year as governor, the state put together a 2.1 billion dollar economic stimulus plan to incentivize private development. The two billion dollars worked like a charm. It leveraged an additional nineteen billion in private investment, making for a total of twenty-one billion dollars of development that went into the state that wouldn't have otherwise.

One of our biggest programs was directly inspired by Al and the day we met on that vacant site. "Business in Our Sites" was a 300 million dollar pool of money that was paid for by the state borrowing economic development bonds. To be eligible for a portion of the pool, the county, city, or township that applied for the loan had to have a site in mind that was vacant and environmentally challenged.

As an example: if the city of Pittsburgh spent four million in cleanup to get a site shovel-ready for development, "Business in Our Sites" would cut Pittsburgh a four million dollar check. Pittsburgh signed a contract, promising to repay the money through the site's property taxes or through the site's sale, and "Building in Our Sites" recycled the repaid loan into a new project, creating a cycle of reinvestment.

All in all, "Business in Our Sites" created close to a half billion dollars' worth of cleanup and development, which was responsible for seven or eight thousand new jobs. All of that job creation resulted from one meeting with one vertically challenged giant. Al Boscov convinced me to do "Business in our Sites" in less than an hour by showing me a site most people would have overlooked or called urban blight.

Over my eight years as governor, that scenario repeated itself six or seven times. Al would call and say, "I have something you need to see, come to Reading!"

If passion was his secret to success, boy, was he passionate about his hometown, and boy, could he sell the city of Reading.

A good salesmen discovers the sweet spot for the person he's selling. Al learned I loved food. He loved food, too, so every time I came to Reading, he would get me a delicious meal—lunch or dinner—and then he would get me for whatever project he was selling. He was nonstop. He always had a new idea, along with new stories to sell me on the importance of the project.

We did the following projects together in Reading: the GoggleWorks Center for the Arts, the GoggleWorks Apartments, the Imax in Entertainment Square, and Reading's first four-star hotel. All of these projects he developed out of love for the city and the country that gave him, his father, and his family an opportunity to succeed.

The only time he ever asked for a personal favor was during the financial crisis when Boscov's went into bankruptcy. Even then, he didn't ask for himself. He asked for the people who worked at the company and for the surrounding communities that would have been affected by Boscov's closing. No one thought he could pull it off. But he did. No Boscov's closed in Pennsylvania, and the state and the federal government have gotten back the majority of their investments. That was the only time he ever asked me for anything that was remotely connected to himself. But he didn't ask for himself. He asked so he could save thousands of jobs.

Tom Hinkle

Following 9/11, there became an impetus to create data centers in Eastern Pennsylvania; the idea was to protect against an event of such catastrophic proportion, so even if something happened in New York, Wall Street would have backup centers out of state.

At the time, I was the vice president of technology at Boscov's; because I was the technology guy, Albert invited me to a meeting for a project called, "Wall Street West." A tech company was presenting their plan to the governor and to various businessmen on how to build a fiber optic network out of 60 Hudson, which is a demark point for fiber networks from Manhattan into Eastern Pennsylvania.

After the meeting, Albert wanted my thoughts.

I told him, "Honestly, I don't think it's a good idea."

He wanted to know why not.

I said, "If the state spends one hundred twenty million dollars on a fiber network, there's going to be about eighty million of that spent in New Jersey, and that's Pennsylvania taxpayer money."

He said, "What would you do?"

"I'd buy the old, abandoned GPU building by the Reading Airport. It has state-of-the-art data centers and a built-in fiber network that's already connected to 60 Hudson."

So that's what he did. Albert bought the old GPU building. Remember that this was in 2005-2006. Albert was supposedly retired. He was running a nonprofit, and now he was starting a new company, DirectLink. He brought me on board to help run the back-up centers out of the GPU building. Eleven hundred people now work in that building. They're tenants—not employees—but that's a lot of people who now have a workplace, which brings us to 2008.

While Albert was away from Boscov's, the store invested in ten new stores, unfortunately, at the worst time; the housing and financial crisis occurred, which sent Boscov's into bankruptcy.

When a company enters bankruptcy, bankruptcy court requires the company to enter a binding stalking horse agreement to be considered for competitive auction. A stalking horse agreement is made with an initial purchaser (the stalking horse), who provides an initial bid. In the case of Boscov's, the stalking horse wished to sell off all of Boscov's assets, which would mean closing every store. To make it worse, Boscov's is an anchor store, so its closing would impact all of the malls where there are Boscov's and all of the people who worked even nearby.

Around the time that the stalking horse bid went in, Albert and I were at DirectLink. My office was down the hall from his.

He came to my door, and he said, "Tom, I need to talk to you."

Was I in trouble?

I said, "Come in."

He stood in my doorway, almost with tears in his eyes.

"I'm going back to Boscov's."

"What for?"

He said, "The company is in trouble. If I don't do something, nine thousand people will lose their jobs."

I told him, "Do what you have to do."

Of course, you know what he did. He saved the company.

Sandy Zervanos

To this day, if you go down to the infants department at the Berkshire Mall, you'll notice a birdcage. That birdcage belongs to Willy, the Boscov's store parrot. He's been with the store for decades. Around the time of the bankruptcy, Willy would have been maybe fifty or sixty years old.

One day, Mr. Boscov brought a group of bankers and investors

to the Berkshire Mall, as a way of saying to them, "Look at that—Isn't it wonderful? Look at how great this store is. We need to save it!"

I happened to be down in the children's department at the time. I'd worked in fine jewelry since the Berkshire Mall opened in 2002, and I had a few pieces of kids' jewelry to rearrange. All of a sudden, Mr. B came by with this group of bankers in their dark suits.

He told them, "I want to introduce you to Willy."

The bankers looked around. They didn't know where to look or who Willy even was. Mr. Boscov said, "Up there is Willy."

They were right underneath Willy's birdcage.

Mr. B said, "Say hello, Willy."

Willy didn't say anything. The bankers didn't know what to think, so Mr. B said again, "Say hello to the nice men, Willy."

Still nothing.

"Say hello, Willy."

Finally, the bird said, "Hello."

The men were delighted. They simply loved it.

Mr. B said, "Good, Willy, now see if you can say this. Tell the nice men...," and then Mr. B threw his voice as if he were the parrot, "*We need more money. We need more money.*"

I just cracked up. Everyone in the area cracked up, too. To hear him throw his voice and pretend to be a parrot was one thing, but that he would do this in front of a group of investors who he was trying to impress....

He was just so down-to-earth. If he didn't already have them in his pocket, I'm sure that did the trick.

Mel Blum

When the company was in bankruptcy, I spent a lot of time with Albert while he put together the financial package to save the company. I'd been driving Albert and Eunice for the past eleven years. I've never heard a couple their age use so many terms of endearment. Albert would call Eunice "honey," "sweetheart," "darling," "she's my cutie pie," or simply "Eunie" (You-nee).

Sometimes, Eunice would call to see how he was and what he was eating. He'd say "I have an apple in my hand" while we were pulling into a parking lot to get ice cream. I'm sorry, Eunice, but he also liked his McDonald's and a lot of fast food. Sometimes Albert would give me a fake title so I could accompany him into meetings.

I was the head of this or that, but really he just liked my company. We spent a lot of time together, driving across the state and over meals.

One day, we had to go to New Jersey because there was an issue with the Atlantic City freeholders. If the freeholders voted against Boscov's, the Atlantic City store would end up in the hands of its creditors.

On the way home, after a taxing day, Albert was on the phone in the passenger seat instead of in the back where he usually sat with his Boscov's baskets and all of his paperwork. When he hung up, he tried to get his papers, but he couldn't reach them, so he said, "Mel, pull over."

We were driving at seventy miles per hour along the Atlantic City expressway. I found a nice clear spot, got on my flashers, and

pulled over. If you're familiar with the Atlantic City expressway, in some places it's raised, and there's a green slope running down the side. Before I was at a complete stop, the front door opened. He was that eager to work.

Albert proceeded to fall and roll down the side of the highway, and I mean roll— five or six times. You can imagine my shock.

Before I could even get out of the car, he jumped up, ran up the hill, opened the back door, got his paperwork, hopped in front, and said, "Mel, let's go." I don't think anything could stop him.

Tom Hinkle

When Mel wasn't available, Vivian enlisted me to drive Albert to the various communities where there were Boscov's. From each of those communities, basically, Albert begged for money. That's the truth. That's how he saved the company. We drove from county to county, state to state, and he asked for help. This was in the middle of the financial crisis when nothing was getting done. No one knew what to expect from the economy; yet he and the Boscov family put money back into the company.

He wouldn't have been able to do it if it wasn't for the support of the federal and the local government and, most importantly, the support of the communities where there are Boscov's.

I remember we drove to Atlantic City three times. The third time, the county freeholders were ready to vote against the store receiving the funding.

That day, close to two-hundred people showed up.

Maybe half of them were Boscov's coworkers. The other half were employees from the Egg Harbor Township mall. Those couple hundred people told the freeholders, "If you don't do this, a lot of us will lose our jobs."

At the time, Atlantic City was Boscov's biggest store in dollar volume. If it wasn't for those people who showed up and said, "Listen..." I don't know if that store would exist today.

Sandy Valgus

In 2008, Albert held a meeting for all of the coworkers at East. The financing had only recently gone through to buy back the company. When he stepped behind the podium, everyone in the auditorium applauded him.

He told us, "I appreciate the applause, and I appreciate everything, but it's not over yet."

He then told us about how embarrassed and ashamed he was having to buy back his name. As he talked, his eyes got teary, and his cheeks sunk. He looked so frail behind the podium.

In the moment, I don't think I thought of it, but Albert always reminded me of my father. They even have the same birthday. I remember Albert once helped my father replace a defective toy for a grandchild.

I have so many memories at the store. I remember Albert singing in the hall. He always had time to have a conversation with you.

He was just a regular Joe really, and I loved that about him—that he wasn't some billion dollar businessman. I guess I just couldn't stand to see him up there pouring his heart out to all these people. When he started crying and couldn't go on, something came over me.

I screamed out, "We love you, Albert."

Everyone in the room cheered.

He stepped down from the podium, and he kissed my forehead. Then he resumed talking business—about what we were going to do to bring back sales and about his whole big plan. At that moment, I think everyone in the store and everyone who worked for him realized he was just a little human being, and he had feelings like any of us.

There wasn't a dry eye in the place.

Barbara Zerbe

At the Meriden store opening in Connecticut, I saw him and wanted to say, "Thank you" for bailing out the company. If it wasn't for him, we wouldn't be here. I wouldn't have a job. I think everyone here should remember that. So I stopped him.

He said, "Hiya, how are you?" and he shook my hand.

I told him who I was, and that I work in curtain and drapes at North.

He said, "I know where you work."

I thought, "Of all the people employed by him, there's no way he knows..." But he just had a way of making you feel important.

I said, "I want to thank you."

He wouldn't take any credit. When I said, "Thank you," he instead asked me, "How are you, and how's your department?"

I repeated myself, "I really just want to say thank you for what you did."

He said "Well, you know..." He put an arm around me, "But how are you?"

He still wouldn't take any credit for himself.

Valerie Pentz

I was a first-time home buyer. I had just put in to buy a house when the bankruptcy happened. They held on to my mortgage. They weren't going to approve me. When they heard Mr. B was buying back the company, all of a sudden everything went through.

They even told me, "We were worried because it was your main job."

I'm eternally grateful to my second grandfather. I didn't have many one-on-ones with Mr. B, but he was just that figure whom I always knew I could count on. I've been with Boscov's North for thirty-five years. I'm now in handbags. Before that, I was the main manager of Tobacco and Lottery/Ticketmaster.

I was the store manager at the Danville store when things took a turn for the worse in 2008. My wife and I both lost our jobs on the same day, but we never gave up hope to come back to the family.

We went off with J.C. Penney for a few years. At one point, I got transferred back to Pennsylvania with Penneys. Beckey and I took a drive to East, hoping to see Mr. Boscov and say hello.

In the reception office, Vivian said, "Just go in and say hi. He will be glad to see you."

We did, and he stopped his meeting for twenty minutes to ask us about our lives and what was going on. When I was leaving, I bumped into Ed Elko. He asked if we ever thought about coming back.

I said "every day."

In less than two weeks, I'm interviewing with Mr. Boyer and Ed Elko for a position.

I have tons of funny moments like everyone else, but a recent one sticks out. When I came back to the company, I helped open the Ohio store. During that time, a customer I was working with went up to Mr. Boscov to say hello and tell him about the great service I gave them.

They didn't know my position or anything about me. Mr. Boscov talked to them for a few moments, then said, "I hired David when he was in diapers."

I tell everyone that story.

Barbara Yousaitis

Mr. Boscov was in the store a couple of years ago thanking us for working on Thanksgiving. Everyone was really sluggish in the morning, so to get people excited he said, "Let's hear stories! Let's hear stories!" No one was really talking, so I said, "I have a story." And he said, "Oh, good, good."

He had me come up and I said, "I just want to tell you a wonderful memory I have growing up with Boscov's. When I was a little girl growing up in Pennside, the big thing at Easter was the Boscov's egg drop. You would send helicopters to all the different playgrounds, and all the kids would run over to the playground with our mothers and wait to hear that helicopter coming over the mountain. It would get lower and lower. Suddenly you could see the Easter Bunny in the helicopter, throwing out styrofoam eggs. The eggs would hit the ground, and we'd go running and pick them up. To get a prize, you had to go to Boscov's and put your eggs under a black light that showed what you won."

As I was telling him this story, he exclaimed, "I remember that!"

I said, "I wish you'd do that again, and he said, "I just might," and he handed me this dollar and signed it, "One good idea."

I cherish this dollar.

Every Thanksgiving I worked, and people used to say, "I can't believe you have to work on Thanksgiving." And I'd say, "It's one day, and I wouldn't have this job if it weren't for him."

After the bankruptcy, we didn't know what would happen. He went out to every store, and had meetings with everyone, reassuring us that we were going to be okay. Because of the economy, he asked us if we would work on Thanksgiving. He said, "I just want four hours of your time. We'll come in the morning. You'll go home in time for dinner."

And we did that. We'd come in at six and leave at one. It's changed with competitive retailers. We now work longer hours, but I will continue to work Thanksgiving because of him. That's a small thing to ask for all he did. You know, I really miss him. I miss him.

I never had long conversations with Albert, but the little things impressed me. I'm the men's suit manager at Neshaminy and over the years, I helped open twelve stores. Whenever we opened a store, he went around and shook hands with literally every employee all the way down to the guy sweeping the floor. That's the owner of the company.

What's that tell you—that he thanked each and every one of us for our work?

Not everybody takes the time to do that, and it means a lot to people. It makes folks feel appreciated.

Now some people have appreciation, but they don't take the time or make the effort to let you know it. There's a difference between having appreciation and showing it, and he knew that.

A few months before he passed, he was with Karl, our store manager.

I walked over to Albert, and I said, "How are you feeling, boss?"

I had never asked how he felt before.

He said, "I feel good."

I shook his hand and said, "Well, you look great."

He hugged me and, as he held me, he said to Karl, "This is my baby. My baby."

That's what my father used to call me. Whenever people ask me about Albert, I tell them that he was the second greatest man who's ever lived, next to my father.

That's how much I thought of him.

When our family first heard of my grandpa's cancer diagnosis, I was just starting my second semester of junior year at Boston University. Immediately after the terrible news, I went back home to see him and to spend time with the whole family. This routine continued every weekend until February, when my mom called and told me that the upcoming weekend would most likely be my final time seeing him. My last day with Granddaddy Al was filled with the usual laughter, fun, and happiness that occurs when you are around him. We both knew that it would be our last time together, but his optimism and ability to never let anything bring him down allowed us to enjoy our time together, rather than grieve.

Throughout the period of time when he was sick, what I admired most was the fact that he always stayed positive. Although death was inevitable, he kept working to make sure Boscov's would have its best year ever, and he made sure to enjoy his time with the family.

I never once saw him accept his fate; even the last day I saw him he was talking about beating cancer. I knew and the family knew that it was an impossible cancer to beat, but his "nothing is impossible" attitude made us all want to believe that the impossible would actually happen.

When he died, I remember returning to Boston from the memorial service and feeling lost. I had lost my hero, my grandpa, and the best person I will ever know. I didn't know how I would ever recover. My friends were there to support me, but nothing they could do could truly help; it was not until I got a call from my cousin Josh that I started to see the light. Josh asked if I would like to help put a book together about Granddaddy (the book you are now finishing reading), and then he sent me a document with all of the condolence letters that our family received. While reading through those hundreds and hundreds of stories, I could finally smile.

Everyone's stories made me realize I was not the only one in mourning. I no longer felt alone. Everyone who knew him was trying to figure out how to carry on after his passing.

After finishing the stories, all I wanted to do was hear more.

As you now know, my cousins and I spent the summer collecting stories. Some silly. Some emotional. Together, they show who he was. Every new story we heard made him feel alive to me and filled a void in my life. The stories taught me what it means "to Boscov" on any given day: how to emulate him while being my best self.

It is our hope that when others read this book, they too will be inspired to "Boscov." The greatest value our grandfather wished to pass on to his children and grandchildren was "to give back." He felt indebted to the country that gave his father an opportunity and wished we, too, would remember that debt. If you would like to contribute to the better world that Al Boscov envisioned, it is as easy as giving back to your community, wherever you live, to whatever charity or cause is close to your heart.

All proceeds from the sale of this book go to the nonprofit our grandfather started, Our City Reading, which seeks to revitalize the city of Reading, Pennsylvania. You can learn more about Our City Reading at ourcityreading.org.

a big thank you to the city of reading and beyond

Acknowledgements

My cousins and I owe a debt of gratitude to so many people. In chronological order, to Joanne Barker who came up to me at the memorial service (accompanied by her grandson Reese) and said, "There should be a book of memories about Albert;" to Craig Hafer who seconded the idea by introducing us to Walter Woolwine, Christopher D'Angelo, Michael Doyle, and Jan Abramowicz of the Reading Eagle, who printed the book you're holding now; to Abby Ryder and Jessica Santucci, whose charming artwork brought Granddaddy's spirit alive on the page; and to the GoggleWorks Center for the Arts for fostering talented artists like them.

Thanks also to Randall Brown (my uncle and Jonah's dad), who turned an unedited manuscript of text into a book that's a joy to read; to my mother Ruth, for scanning hundreds of photos; to Anna DeBlasio for her editing prowess; to Scott Esterbrook for taking on the (no longer) thankless task of handling the paperwork; and to Jim Boscov, Melissa Antrim, and everyone at Boscov's for their enthusiasm and support every step of the way.

This book would be largely empty if it weren't for everyone at Boscov's East, North, the Berkshire Mall, Neshaminy, Wilkes Barre, the Coventry Mall, Egg Harbor Township, and DirectLink—who shared their stories with us—and for everyone who contributed a memory or photograph.

To the thousands who shared condolences following our grandfather's passing, your kind words made a trying time easier to bear. Your stories allowed us to live with our Granddaddy Al a few extra days, a few more hours, and to learn lessons from him that we will carry with us for the rest of our lives. There are so many wonderful stories that we couldn't fit into this book, which is why we will continue sharing as many stories and photographs as we can on our Facebook page: Memories of Al.

If you have a story you wish to share, you can always send it in on Facebook or by email at memoriesofal@boscovs.com.

~ *Josh Aichenbaum* (with his cousins, Jonah and Amelia looking over his shoulder, giving him the thumbs-up)

Al Boscov's grandkids on a family trip, circa June 2003.

Artists' Bios

Abby Ryder is a printmaker and illustrator from Reading,  Pennsylvania. She graduated from the University of Pittsburgh's studio arts program in 2013 and currently maintains a studio practice at the Goggleworks Center for the Arts in Reading. She is interested in self-portraits, doodling, and hanging out with her cat. You can view more of Abby's work online at www.abbyryderart.com.

Jess Santucci is a freelance illustrator and graphic designer currently  living in southeastern Pennsylvania. She received her BFA in illustration from Pennsylvania College of Art and Design in 2015. She specializes in mixing the charming with the macabre to create her own brand of intricate paintings and whimsical characters. Her work focuses on exploring the impermanence of the physical self in contrast with the wild world that surrounds us. She is heavily influenced by nature, folklore, and the occult. When Jess isn't painting, she can be found curled up on her couch watching horror movies and knitting. More of her work can be seen at her website: jsantucciart.com.